A Right to Play

A Right to Play

PROCEEDINGS OF THE AMERICAN ASSOCIATION
FOR THE CHILD'S
RIGHT TO PLAY
SEPTEMBER 17-20, 1992
DENTON, TEXAS

Edited by
Marcy Guddemi
Tom Jambor

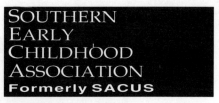

SOUTHERN
EARLY
CHILDHOOD
ASSOCIATION
Formerly SACUS

LITTLE ROCK, ARKANSAS

Southern Early Childhood Association
P.O. Box 56130
Little Rock, AR 72215-6130

ISBN 0-942388-09-7

Printed in the United States of America

Contents

Preface

The American Association for the Child's Right to Play, known as IPA/USA, is proud to present the proceedings from Play: A Daily Minimum Requirement, the triennial IPA/USA national conference hosted by The University of North Texas on Sept. 17-20, 1992. More than 100 presenters from the United States, New Zealand, Australia, Japan, and Sweden delivered 74 papers on aspects of play: child development, education, recreation, safety, design, habitats, play therapy, international play opportunities, advocacy and much more. Of the 37 papers submitted to the IPA/USA conference proceedings committee, the editors selected 20 papers for inclusion in this publication.

The conference was co-sponsored by 10 organizations; more than 25 people helped plan, organize, and work on conference committees; 435 participants attended. The conference had three keynote addresses, a preconference Play-Day, playground and play therapy center tours, concurrent sessions, exhibitors, and plenty of playful activities for participants. We would like to thank everyone involved, with special acknowledgements to the following:

Co-Sponsors
Region VI Head Start Association
Texas Association For the Education of Young Children
Southern Early Childhood Association
Texas Head Start Association
Denton County AEYC
University of North Texas College of Education
University of Alabama at Birmingham
Texas Association of Health, Physical Education, Recreation and Dance
University of Oklahoma-Center for Child and Family Development
KinderCare Learning Center, Inc.

Conference Co-Chairpersons
Mike Bell, University of North Texas
Ann O'Bar, University of Oklahoma Center for Child and Family Development

Keynote Session Speakers
Garry L. Landreth, Ph.D.
    Director, Center for Play Therapy
    University of North Texas
Robin Moore, Dip. Arch., M.C.P.
    Professor of Landscape Architecture and Program Director, Center for Accessible Housing, North Carolina State University at Raleigh
Joe L. Frost, Ed.D.
    Catherine Mae Parker Centennial Professor of Curriculum and Instruction, University of Texas at Austin

Conference Committees
Accommodations: Ann O'Bar
Administrative Assisstant: Jill Fox
Audiovisual: Christi Turner, Lisa Rankin
Conference Evaluation: Kathy Fite
Conference Packets: Carol Hagen
Exhibits: Pam Fleege, Jill Fox
Facilitators/Hospitaility: Nancy Pyle, Arminta Jacobson, Denton Association for the Education of Young Children
Planning: Mike Bell, Marcy Guddemi, Tom Jambor, Ann O'Bar, Randy Smith
PlayDay: Tere Holmes, Loretta McAlister, Sue Adams, Dana Gomez, Marie Lawrence, Pam Meason
Playground Tours: Jim Dempsey, Eric Strickland
Proceedings: Marcy Guddemi, Tom Jambor
Program: Marcy Guddemi, Rose Winkler
Resolutions: Ann O'Bar, Randy Smith
Youth Performances: Paula Weaver

IPA/USA Board of Directors
President: Marcy Guddemi
Treasurer: Jim Campbell
Secretary: Randy Smith
Members at Large: Jim Dempsey, Ann O'Bar
Past President: Tom Jambor
Member Development: Sunny Davidson
Parliamentarian/International Liaison: Robin C. Moore
Historian: Paul Hogan
Newsletter/Membership: Nancy Eletto

Publisher
Southern Early Childhood Association

Managing Editor
Elizabeth F. Shores

Proofreaders
Jane Alexander
Dee English

Secretarial and Administrative Support
Lora Capps
Rose Winkler

IPA/USA (the American affiliate of the International Association for the Child's Right To Play) is a professional organization for educators, architects, landscape architects, physical educators, teachers, child care workers, city planners, pediatricians, parents, and park and recreation people. Our mission is to uphold and support the child's right to play as guaranteed by the 1959 Declaration on the Rights of the Child and further supported by the Convention on the Rights of the Child, Article 31 (1990). We believe that play, like vitamins, is an essential part of life and without adequate amounts of play one suffers. Hence, the conference theme *Play: A Daily Minimum Requirement* was selected. The conference mission and subsequent mission of this book are to spread the message that play is a right of children.

MARCY GUDDEMI
President
IPA/USA

TOM JAMBOR
Past President
IPA/USA

September, 1993

Introduction

"Mankind owes the child the best it has to give."
United Nations Declaration on the Rights of the Child, 1959

MARCY GUDDEMI
TOM JAMBOR

For more than three decades the Declaration on the Rights of the Child has granted children the right to food and survival, to shelter and protection, to development and education, to freedom and participation — and the right to leisure and play. Even though 123 countries signed the Convention on the Rights of the Child at the World Summit for Children (October 1992), ratifying their official intent to make these rights legally binding, children in even the most affluent nations are not obtaining their basic rights and needs. The International Association for the Child's Right to Play was organized in 1961 to focus on one particular right: the child's right to play.

Play is very important to children for many reasons. Play is a basic need along with nutrition, health, shelter and education. While play defies definition, we do know that it is instinctive, voluntary, and spontaneous, done purely for pleasure, and has no predetermined result. Play helps children develop physically, emotionally, socially, and intellectually. Play is a way that children can communicate and express themselves. Play is a means of learning about life itself. Play is universal, knowing no national or cultural boundaries. Unfortunately, we also find that play, a crucial element in human development, is becoming scarce.

Several factors today are causing an erosion of children's play opportunities at the same time that they negatively affect children's growth, development, and learning.

The first factor is continuing poverty. Increasing numbers of children are living with inadequate provision for survival and development because of poverty and substandard living conditions. Many children are forced to work at life-sustaining chores such as child-rearing, food preparation, planting and harvesting, and manual labor as soon as they are old enough to follow directions or to understand that if they don't work they will be beaten. Poverty forces children to be miniature adults during the preschool years. For many children, both the opportunity and even the hope for play are nonexistent.

In the inner cities of developed countries, conditions are very similar to developing economies. Children are rearing younger children, performing manual labor for drug money, and begging for food rather than playing. Interestingly, if play were possible for any of these children of poverty, the streets in the villages of underdeveloped countries would actually be safer for play than those in a majority of America's inner cities.

The second factor is changing cultural values. While there is no time for play in underdeveloped societies and inner cities, there is an indifference toward the importance of play in developed societies. Whereas, children traditionally have been shielded from adult responsibilities and encouraged to play into their late teens or early twenties, now play is increasingly frowned on by parents who want their children to work and learn at the earliest possible moment rather than play. Society believers that play is frivolous while work is productive. Even the great Maria Montessori called the children's activities in her preschool "work."

According to both David Elkind (*The Hurried Child*, 1982) and Neil Postman (*The Disappearance of Childhood*, 1982), childhood as an institution is rapidly disappearing in the United States and other Western nations. Children's weekly itineraries are too often jammed with music lessons, scout meetings, little league, soccer, dance lessons, etc. to allow children the time to play and to just be children. Today children are also being thrust into adulthood by wearing mature or sexually provocative clothes, by being exposed to sexual and violent situations on TV and radio, and by being forced to handle growing societal stress, such as divorce, job loss, war, and racial injustice. This is particularly true in urban centers.

Another cultural trend is the increased dependence on television, media, and video games as part of the daily routine. Preschool children watch an average of 4.5 hours of television alone daily. Passively viewing television and other media is a double negative on the child's right to play. Not only can children be adversely affected by what they view, but also time spent watching television and playing video games could be time spent genuinely playing.

The third factor is inadequate space to play. Children's play spaces have been sorely ignored and neglected. Many cities in their rush to build banks, hotels, malls, and suburbs have forgotten the needs of children. Children need safe spaces in which to play and to be creative. Developers are not given incentives to build play spaces into their designs. Only nine countries have some form of national standards for children's play spaces in residential environments. Children growing up in cities of high density have as little as four square meters of living and playing space per family. Research also shows that the higher the floor of residential occupancy, the less children play. Even suburbs, the answer to crime-ridden and crowded inner cities, have few sidewalks and few play spaces devoted to children. Children can't even walk or ride a bicycle to a friend's house to play. Parents complain that all play experiences must, therefore, be prearranged and require a chauffeur. Residential developments that do have play or recreation space cater mainly to the adults' needs — clubhouses, tennis, exercise rooms — not to children's needs. Where are children's playgrounds?

The state of America's playgrounds is de-plorable at best. Children's playgrounds, when they do exist, are all too often in serious need to maintenance and lack developmental value altogether. Children are not only at risk of losing important play spaces, but also are at physical risk. Each year more than 200,000 children are injured seriously enough on playgrounds in America to warrant medical attention. Approximately four out of five of these injuries result from falls and impacts to non-resilient surfaces, with about one-half causing head and neck injuries and an average of one death each month. While statistics and publications abound that pinpoint dangers, we often do very little remediation of playground problems to lower children's risk of accident and injury.

Sound knowledge, awareness, and priorities must be obtained and established by responsible adults if safe and developmentally appropriate playgrounds are going to be provided our children. IPA/USA historian Paul Hogan puts it this way:

> When our car has a funny tic, we rush it to the garage mechanic. We have trained inspectors to make sure our elevators run smoothly and safely. Every public fire extinguisher in America has a little tag on it with the inspector's initials and date of last inspection. Our boiler rooms are protected by boiler inspectors, our airplanes protected by the FAA, our ships by the Coast Guard, ad infinitum, ad nausem. How many years ago was your playground really inspected by a competent, well-trained person? Why are our boats and elevators more imprtant to us than our children?

Recently, Ernest Boyer (*Ready to Learn*, 1922) commented, "Children give life to neighborhoods, yet neighborhoods are giving nothing back to children."

The final factor is the overemphasis on "work" and underemphasis on "play" in elementary schools and preschools. Many schools and learning settings force young children to sit all day with dittos, paper-and-pencil tasks, and rote memorization exercises. It is often forgotten that children learn through play. They need to touch, play with, and manipuate objects and materials in their environment to develop cognitive constructs for optimal intellectual growth. Indoor play, as well as outdoor recess play periods, have been squeezed out of the curriculum and abolished by all too many schools.

Play, in its fullest potential, helps children grow and learn intellectual skills. It also enhances social skills as children work out differences of perspective through sharing, cooperating, and turn taking. Children also grow and learn emotionally and gain confidence and self-respect through their successful play activities. And, of course, play helps children grow physically as they gain coordination, strength, ability, and other basic physical skills. In total, play is one of the most important requirements for developing a healthy child.

As we look at what we now know about the history of play, the value and benefits of play, what conferences such as the 1992 IPA/USA conference taught us, and the state of today's society, we understand that perhaps *granting* children the right to food and survival, to shelter and protection, to development and education, to freedom and participation — and the right to leisure and play — was the easy part. *Guaranteeing* children those same rights is much more difficult. Our responsibility to the children of the world is to give them "the best we have to give"; to give children the opportunity to be children in their early years, and, to give children the opportunity to play.

Part I
Children's Play: A Health Capsule for the 21st Century

As might be expected, the opinions, attitudes and projections concerning the child's right to play as this decade closes and we approach the 21st century are numerous. Advocates abound, as well documented at the 1992 IPA/USA conference, Play: A Daily Minimum Requirement. The participants spoke to each other and with each other. They presented a well-documented array of problems and suggested an array of solutions. But, are the messages regarding the child's right to play going beyond the presentations, and this book? Is the message reaching those who are politically, socially, and economically affluent enough to help implement the charges for change on a large scale? To bring about change within the greater population is indeed a challenge for any advocacy group. We must continue to reach out to those who can make a difference, hold on tight, and not let go until we have met all children's needs.

IPA/USA has nurtured an interdisciplinary group of professionals and practitioners to be strong advocates for the child's right to play. Our leaders have emerged from this base to form and focus policies that can and will have a serious impact on play in our society. The keynote addresses and commentary presented in this section are by leaders in the IPA/USA advocacy movement to better chidlren's play environments. **Tom Jambor**, Ed.D., past president of IPA/USA from The University of Alabama at Birmingham, and **Marcy Guddemi**, Ph.D., current president of IPA/USA from the corporate offices of KinderCare, lead off this series of addresses with a core of issues fundamental to the 1992 conference theme and mission.

The papers that follow, presented as keynote addresses by three international leaders and experts in the field of play, answer different questions. They agree, however, that play is the answer. **Garry L. Landreth**, Ph.D. director of the Center of Play Therapy at the University of North Texas discusses the emotional healing capacity of play. **Robin C. Moore**, Dip. Arch., M.C.P., School of Design, North Carolina State University at Raleigh and International President of IPA, summarizes the legal implications of the "child's right to play." **Joe L. Frost**, Ed.D., Catherine Mae Parker Centennial Professor of Curriculum and Instruction at the University of Texas at Austin and past president of the American Association for the Child's Right To Play, concludes with a chronology of the study of play and playscapes over the last few decades.

Chapter 1
Can Our Children Play?

Tom Jambor
Marcy Guddemi

TJ: What play opportunities does the future hold for our children and our children's children? If we could look into the future, would we see even the most basic elements essential for play? Will children have a heathy attitude and a strong motivation toward play? Will they indeed be healthy enough to physically participate in play if opportunities are available?

To think of play as "a health capsule for children of the future," an examination of the child of today is necessary. Looking at the child physically, it appears our nation is producing a generation of kids who have a high probability of becoming sedentary adults and developing serious health problems. As the 1980's began, only 43% of elementary school children could pass National Physical Fitness Program tests. When the present decade began only 32% could pass the same tests. The physical fitness statistics were appalling. Some examples: 35% of boys and 70% of girls couldn't do more than one pull-up; 30% of boys and 50% of girls couldn't run a mile in less than 10 minutes; 25% of boys and 55% of girls couldn't do more than one push-up. These figures may be related to other statistics that show that our children are heavier. Today 15% to 20% of American children are classifed as "fat." Since 1970, obesity has increased 54% among children ages 6 to 11. And, it is sad to note, boys 10 years and older weigh an average of 14 pounds more now than they did 10 years ago.

The American Academy of Pediatrics also reports that 50% of children are not getting enough exercise to develop healthy hearts and lungs, and that 40% of five- to eight-year-olds show at least one factor for heart-disease: elevated blood pressure, high cholesterol, and/or

physical inactivity. In addition, less activity means children will be more susceptible to serious health problems in addition to heart disease, like hypertension, diabetes, psychological disorders, impaired heart tolerance, and other related ailments as they move into adulthood. What will the statistics look like in the next decade? What has happened to all too many of the children? Why have they become more sedentary in their lifestyles? Why have the physical actions and the physical encounters of play with peers and environments been reduced? What has taken place? Could one or more of the following be part of the answer?

- A greater reliance on motorized transportation
- A greater indulgence in excessive television viewing
- A greater emphasis on technological games
- A past negative attitude about girls who favored playing sports
- A growing number of "latch-key" children whose parents greatly restrict outdoor play after school
- A growing number of parents who restrict outdoor play because of of justified fears of violence to their children — even in their own neighborhoods and back yards
- A greater emphasis on expanded academic programs that have either eliminated or severely limited "recess" from children's daily schedule
- A growing urbanization over the past 20 years that has slowly, but methodically, squeezed out the "natural" play spaces utilized by children — and increasing fear among parents that natural places are dangerous
- The formal play environments provided our children are unappealing or unsafe because of the lack of proper maintenance, and therefore, go unused Anyone working with and for chil-

dren could undoubtedly expand this list. We have a nation of children at risk of losing the opportunity and the right to play.

Those who attended the 1992 conference and those who will use this book are a unique breed, for they look to play as an answer. They look to the concepts and the numerous applications associated with play as the foundation that supports healthy children:

• who have a zeal and curiosity for learning;
• who can handle the ordinary stresses of everyday life;
• who can feel comfortable as social beings;
• who are able to participate physically to their optimal ability, and
• who just feel good, happy, and competent in what they do.

Play, sounds so simple and frivolous but is so complex and fundamental to the whole child's very being.

The fine presentations found in this book are clear testimony to our commitment to play and the effect it can have on children's healthy development. But the conference and book are only samples of our efforts and ambitions. We must expand and shape our play philosophies, our play designs, and our play applications into well-developed policies within our respective fields to ensure every child the right to play.

MG: Dr. Jambor has addressed the question of whether children will be physically healthy enough to play in the 21st century and posed a profile of children who are at risk of losing their right to play because of changes in society. Because of personal and professional research interests, I want to elaborate on two current 20th century practices that Dr. Jambor touched upon, which are replacing play on a daily basis and thus possibly shaping the future and health of our 21st century children. These are television and inappropriate teaching practices in the early years (birth through age eight). The following is a discussion on how unhealthy and "anti-play" television is for young children and how unhealthy — socially, emotionally, intellectually and physically — it is when children are forced to learn in school settings without play opportunities.

Studies indicate that the average preschool child watches television 4.5 hours a day. Since time spent passively viewing television is time that children are not moving and playing, there are actually several negative consequences:

1. Children miss opportunities to develop physical skills, strength, coordination
2. Children miss opportunities to derive benefits afforded from play experiences
3. Children's behavior may be negatively affected.

Children need many daily opportunities to develop physically. They need to run, jump, pedal, climb, hop, skip, push, pull, throw, kick, step, and crawl. Under normal daily conditions children have plenty of opportunities to develop physically through such activities. However, when children spend a third or more of their waking hours sitting passively in front of a television, they are not under normal conditions. The American Academy of Pediatrics has cited television as a contributor to childhood obesity for two reasons: passivity and increased food intake during television viewing.

Studies focusing on the outcomes of play cite beneficial attributes for young children developed through play. The benefits of play included increased flexibility, increased adaptability, increased problem-solving skills, increased creativity, more advanced levels in Piagetian stages, better verbal skills, better divergent and convergent thinking skills, as well as increased happiness, higher levels of self-concept, and nurturance and sensitivity to others. Children who are heavy viewers of television risk not developing these attributes.

The possible negative effects of television-viewing for susceptible children include increased aggression and anti-social behavior due to violent and war-like themes and characters; decline in obedinece, persistence and tolerance for delay; lower scores on achievement tests; decline in attention span; emulation of inappropriate sexual, occupational, and racial role models; increased desire for television and media toys and other times due to the commercials.

Clearly, it behooves parents of young children to limit and restrict the content of television viewing during the early years in order to prepare children for the 21st century.

Current learning theories and research have indicated that young children (birth through age eight) learn differently than adults and older children. Young children "learn through play." This means that young children develop cognitive constructs and understanding through real, hands-on experiences using all of their senses — touching, smelling, hearing, seeing, and tasting. Children also need opportunities for self-directed learning and encouragment to talk and think. Unfortunately, however, many schools, due to an unrealistic reliance on accountability through test scores, inappropriate teaching philosphy for birth to age eight children, and a misunderstanding of the "work" ethic for children, have eliminated hands-on, playful learning experiences in favor of paper-and-pencil and rote learning activities that can be graded and tabulated. Such learning activities are clearly inappropriate for young learners.

Another common practice in schools today is to limit or eliminate recess. Many school districts have felt the pressure from parents and legislators to raise test scores. The remedy for low test scores in many districts was to increase the minutes of instructional time on task. Unfortunately, more academic minutes meant less minutes for recess. Some school districts even outlawed recess. The irony in this scenario is two-fold. First, children need a break from "academic work." One of the classic theories of play which is still held today states that play rejuvenates, relaxes, and builds more energy. Children need the "break" so that they can go back to class ready to begin again. Second, the elimination of recess ignores that fact that children develop essential skills such as problem-solving, risk-taking, cooperation, social skills, language, physical coordination, flexibility, and adaptability which are all necessary for intellectual growth and development. Interestingly, Japanese schools, which are so often touted as being superior to American schools, give several 30-minutes play breaks throughout the day.

Finally, child development experts including educators, pediatricians and child psychologists know that children learn and grow simultaneously in four interrelated domains — social, emotional, physical, and intellectual. Schools too often focus on intellectual growth at the expense of the other three domains. Play, however, does develop all four domains and is the perfect balance in the total curriculum for young children.

Can we guarantee every child's right to play? The following remarks of the three keynoters, in addition to the preceding commentary, are intended to shape the direction of the child's growth, development, learning and right to play within appropriate play environments for the 21 century.

Chapter 2
The Emotional Healing Benefit of Play

GARRY L. LANDRETH

Although some people have said that space is our last frontier, childhood may in fact be our last frontier. We know so little about the complex intricacies of childhood and are limited in our efforts to discover and understand the meanings in childhood because we are forced to allow children to teach us. Many adults don't want to be taught by children, but we can only learn about children from children. Children bring to the relationship, with us as helpers, rich threads of emotional possibilities with which they weave the tapestries of their personalities. The patters which these emotional possibilities form are affected by the helpers, the kinds of responses the helpers make, and the extent of the helpers' understanding of the child's play.

Play is a Universal Language

There are over 4,000 languages communicated throughout the world (Comrie, 1987). Although play is not listed anywhere as one of these languages, it should be. Children from all parts of the world use play to express themselves. They sometimes communicate with toys as their words and play as their language. During play, children can express what they want to express in any way they wish. Thus interaction during free play can be viewed as a limitless language of self-expression because of the unlimited subtle nuances possible. The absence of specific rules of meaning, such as found in verbal communication, is another contributing factor in play's effectiveness as a language of children.

The universal importance of play to the natural development and wholeness of children has been underscored by the United Nations' proclamation of play as a universal and inalienable right of childhood. Play is the singular central activity of childhood, occurring at all times and in all places. Children do not need to be taught how to play, nor must they be made to play. Play is spontaneous, enjoyable, voluntary, and nongoal-directed. When adult-imposed structure is absent, children naturally, spontaneously, and with great energy express and explore their emotional world through their play. This natural process of experiencing life can be emotionally healing when facilitated by an empathic adult who encourages the child's play through understanding, acceptance, warmth, a feeling of permissiveness, and accurate communication of what is experienced.

Basic Principles for the Play Relationship

The expression of these emotional dimensions of caring by an adult facilitates the child's full expression of the self. When these dimensions are present, the child is free to fully use her creative self. The following eight basic principles are considered essential if the play experience is to be healing.

1. The adult is genuinely interested in the child and develops a warm, caring relationship.
2. The adult experiences unqualified acceptance of the child and does not wish the child were different in some way.
3. The adult creates a feeling of safety and permissiveness in the relationship so the child feels free to explore and express self completely.
4. The adult is always sensitive to the child's feelings and gently reflects those feelings in such a manner that the child develops self-understanding.
5. The adult believes deeply in the child's capacity to act responsibly, unwaveringly respects the child's ability to solve problems, and allows the child to do so.

6. The adult trusts the child's inner direction, allows the child to lead, and resists any urge to direct the child's play or conversation.
7. The adult appreciates the gradual nature of the healing process and does not attempt to hurry the process.
8. The adult establishes only those therapeutic limits which help the child accept personal and appropriate relationship responsibility. (Landreth, 1991, p. 77-78)

If these conditions are present, play enables children to express themselves completely. Nothing is held back because the child can express the self safely through the natural facilitative dimensions of play. Play in this setting does not require an explanation, interpretation, or translation into another language. Play is by the very nature of the activity complete, rather than preparation for something else.

Tenets for Relating to Children

If adults are to make a significant contribution to children's lives, they must make emotional contact with children. Children are persons in their own right. Attainment of some predetermined age or meeting certain criteria is not necessary to qualify for being a person. Personal significance is not limited to or a function of the child's behavior. Therefore, children are worthy of respect because they have worth and dignity as individuals. Children are people. They do not have to earn that distinction.

The emotional healing benefit of play occurs naturally when children are respected as persons by a caring adult who does not interfere with their play. It could be said that the most loving thing an adult can do is not to interfere with a child's play. Such an attitude of respect and caring for the child can be summed up in the following tenets for relating to children.

1. Children are not miniature adults and the therapist does not respond to them as if they were.
2. Children are people. They are capable of experiencing deep emotional pain and joy.
3. Children are unique and worthy of respect. The therapist prizes the uniqueness of each child and respects the person they are.

4. Children are resilient. Children possess a tremendous capacity to overcome obstacles and circumstances in their lives.
5. Children have an inherent tendency toward growth and maturity. They possess an inner intuitive wisdom.
6. Children are capable of positive self-direction. They are capable of dealing with their world in creative ways.
7. Children's natural language is play and this is the medium of self-expression with which they are most comfortable.
8. Children have a right to remain silent. The therapist respects a child's decision not to talk.
9. Children will take the therapeutic experience to where they need to be. The therapist does not attempt to determine when or how a child should play.
10. Children's growth cannot be speeded up. The therapist recognizes this and is patient with the child's developmental process. (Landreth, 1991, p. 50)

Play Facilitates a Sense of Control

Play provides healing for hurts and sadness, breaks down tension, and releases pent-up urges toward self-expression. The activity of play is one of the most important ways in which children learn that their feelings can be safely expressed without reprisal or rejection from others (Cass, 1973). Since play is spontaneous and occurs in a safe environment, it allows children to express strong emotions and to learn to cope with anxieties and conflicts. During play, children feel free to act out inner feelings of fear, anger, or loss that might otherwise become overwhelming (Segal and Segal 1989).

Erickson (1977) believed that children resolve conflicts by reconstructing them in symbolic play. Maslow (1968) observed that though children do not plan or set out to grow, growth takes place, and children express outwardly through play what has taken place and is taking place inwardly.

There are many experiences in childhood in which children feel they have little or no control. Play is children's way of working out accompanying feelings of anxiety and fear and reestablishing some sense of balance and control in their lives. When children have experienced a traumatic event, they will play it out in an effort to gain understanding. For example, a child in a hospital might play out the events of that experience with dolls. In doing so, the child gains a sense of control over the hospital procedures and is freed from thinking that the event is taking place as a punishment. Play is an environment children can control.

It is this sense or feeling of control, rather that actual control of events other than play, which is essential to emotional development and positive mental health. Children may experience environments at home or school that are overly structured and controlling, or interactions in which they are controlled by others, but in unstructured free play, the child is in control, the one who decides what to play, how to play, and the outcome. The activity can be what the child wants it to be. In the safety of play, the child can confront monsters, fantasy characters, and frightening experiences with real people and be in charge of the outcome. Great satisfaction can be experienced in having the story end the way the child chooses.

Through the process of expressing themselves in play, children can learn perseverance, the pleasure of choosing a project alone, self-direction, self-responsibility, and that they, along with their choices, are accepted. In addition, the opportunities to engage in problem solving are limitless. Children also develop the self-discipline necessary to engage in a sustained effort, and the resulting satisfaction is a tremendous boost in building positive self-esteem (Landreth, 1993, p. 45-46)

Play Fosters Self-Discovery

White (1960) maintains that play may be fun, but it is also a serious business in childhood. During play, children build up confidence in dealing with their environment. Bruner (1986) believes play gives children their first and most crucial opportunity to have the courage to think, to talk, and to be themselves. According to Amster (1982), play is an activity children comprehend and in which they are comfortable, their method of communication, and their means of testing, partly incorporating and mastering external realities. Since play provides a nonthreatening environment and a flexible atmosphere, creative thoughts are encouraged as children explore and experiment with a variety of solutions to different problems (Tegano et al., 1989). Play allows this process to proceed on a scale controllable by the child. It is through the process of play that children can consider new possibilities not possible in reality, thus greatly expanding the expression of self.

Through play, children find out what the world is like, try on different roles, and cope with conflicting emotions (Papalia and Olds, 1986). The urge to play is universal, and when thwarted can hamper the joyful path of development and self-discovery that is the calling of every child (Bettelheim, 1987). Only through engaging in the process of play can children express and use the totality of their personality. Thus, children extend the person they are, the self, into the creative expression of play. As children develop an appreciation for their play, they begin to discover and accept self.

Frank (1952) enumerated the ways in which play facilitates these discoveries: children express emotions in play, they express their thoughts in play, they rehearse behaviors in play, they exert their will in play, they move through developmental stages with play, and they learn with play. Everything the child is, does and becomes may at one time or another be demonstrated through play.

Children live in the world of the present, yet many of the experiences they encounter in the adult world are future-oriented and abstract. In order to translate these experiences into terms they can understand, children reenact them through play, enabling them to gain a better understanding of the experiences. Through the process of play, children explore the unfamiliar and develop knowledge that is both experiental/feeling and cognitive. Through play, the unfamiliar becomes familiar. The unfamiliar takes on new meaning and the child's expression of self is enhanced. According to Lee (1969), a child has to experience a thing before he or she can understand it. Play, therefore, facilitates understanding and understanding thus facilitates children's self-expression (Landreth, 1993, p. 44-45)

Children Express Their Emotional World Through Play

The emotional healing power of play is perhaps most dramatically evident in the lives of terminally-ill children. For these children, the significance of play in their lives is even more dramatically evident, as in the case of seven-year-old Ryan, who had terminal cancer. In an effort to save Ryan's life, physicians had amputated his right leg. I became part of his life through play therapy experiences a few months after the surgery.

Ryan was not able to verbally discuss his overpowering feeling of helplessness as he became aware of what he was experiencing. He was able, however, to play out those feelings and experiences. This playing-out is a natural process for children and usually occurs spontaneously in play therapy where the therapist works hard to establish a feeling of permissiveness and acceptance.

In the first play therapy session, Ryan took a 10-inch-tall dinosaur, stuck a toy soldier in the wide open gaping mouth, and with his finger slowly pushed the soldier all the way into the mouth until the soldier fell down the dinosaur's throat into the hollow body. He then stood the dinosaur on the floor and lined up three rows of thirty toy soldiers facing the dinosaur. Ryan very carefully made sure all the weapons were pointed toward the dinosaur, then leaned back and studied the scene for several minutes. Not one shot was fired after all of that strategic placement of soldiers. They just stood there, unexpectedly impotent as they faced the huge dinosaur. The feeling was clear. This was a monster, the enemy within Ryan, an enemy that could not be stopped. The soldiers were powerless, their weapons useless. The monster was too powerful. Ryan did not say one word or make any kind of sound during this entire process and did not need to. I was in touch with him and he was communicating.

This was one of those rare experiences in the living relationship of the playroom when, for a few brief moments, time and the reality of everything outside the fleeting experience of the moment did not exist in consciousness for either one of us. I was sensing Ryan's inner experience, captivated by the awesomeness of the scene before me. A moan of anguish moved slowly through my soul — "He knows. He knows."

During the last month of his life, Ryan was too weak to leave his bed, so I carried my traveling play therapy kit to his home. In one of those sessions, I held a newsprint tablet while Ryan drew a picture of Mickey Mouse with huge hands and 40 fingers thrust outward. He then drew a picture of what he first identified as a buzzard and then changed to a porcupine. It seemed to me that the buzzard represented death and the porcupine represented Ryan's intuitive attempt to ward off what was happening to his body. These were feelings Ryan could not put into words, but he did instinctively play out those feelings in the safety of our play relationship. The playing out of such feelings is a releasing experience for children, promoting inner emotional healing in a way that words cannot.

In our last play therapy session, weak and emaciated, Ryan drew the Mickey Mouse figure again but with a smaller body and much smaller hands. He colored Mickey dark purple and the face looked hollow with very dark eyes. Mickey's face clearly looked like death. Ryan then chose an egg carton from the kit, colored the outside black, and then colored each of the egg cells a bright color. This certainly seemed to represent a coffin, and perhaps Ryan was saying where I am going is a place that is bright and colorful. Although Ryan did not verbally discuss death or dying, he was dramatically communicating that death was near. Two days later Ryan died. From Ryan, I learned that even under the most personnally stressful of circumstances, children can experience the pleasure of playing; they can feel in control even when circumstances seem to be out of control. This is the emotional healing capacity of play (Landreth, 1991).

References

Amster, F. (1982). Differential uses of play in treatment of young children. In G. L. Landreth, Ed., *Play therapy: Dynamics of the process of counseling with children*, pp. 33-42. Springfield, Il.: Charles C. Thomas.

Bettelheim, B. (1987). *A good enough parent*. New York: Vintage.

Bruner, J. (1986). Play, thought, and language.

Prospects: Quarterly Review of Education 16, 77-83.

Cass, J. E. (1973). *Helping children grow through play*. New York: Schocken.

Comrie, B. (1989). *The world's major languages*. New York: Oxford University Press.

Erikson, E. H. (1977). *Childhood and society*. New York: Norton.

Frank, L. (1952). *The fundamental needs of the child*. New York: National Association for Mental Health.

Landreth, G. (1991). *Play therapy: The art of the relationship*. Muncie, Ind.: Accelerated Development.

Landreth, G. (1993). Self-expressive communication of play. In C. E. Schaefer (Ed.), *The therapeutic powers of play*, pp. 41-63. Northvale, N.J.: Jason Aronson.

Lee, C. (1969). *The growth and development of children*. 2nd ed. New York: Longman Group Limited.

Maslow, A. H. (1968). *Toward a psychology of being*. New York: D. Van Nostrand.

Papalia, D. and Olds, S. (1986). *Human development*. New York: McGraw-Hill.

Segal, J. and Segal, Z. (1989). Child's play. *Parents, 64:126.*

Tegano, D. W., Sawyers, J. K. & Moran, J. D. (1989). Problem finding and solving in play: The teacher's role. *Childhood Education, 66:* 92-97.

White, R. W. (1960). Competence and the psychosexual stages of development. In M. R. Jones, Ed., *Nebraska Symposium on Motivation*. Lincoln, Neb.: University of Nebraska.

GARRY L. LANDRETH is regents professor and director of the Center for Play Therapy in the Counselor Education Department at the University of North Texas.

Chapter 3
The Child's Right to Play:
Expressions of Article 31

Robin C. Moore

Introduction: Barriers and Rights

In all societies, children face barriers in one form and another which limit their right to play. Many of these barriers are universal and occur in all countries...street traffic, disabilities, prejudice, indifference, hostile physical environments, and even war. If children are poor or orphaned, the barriers are that much greater.

Poor children in all countries are at a disadvantage. Here in the United States, basic rights such as the right to shelter are yet to be responsibly addressed. At the present time, many thousands of children are homeless and forced to live in makeshift shelters, in temporary accommodation, or even on the streets (Hewlett, 1991). These circumstances clearly limit children's development and educational opportunities drastically. If such a shameful situation exists in the richest country in the world, what hope is there for the child's right to play—something that is fairly regarded as less important than the right to decent housing?

The only response must recognize children for what they are: developmental beings. All children will play, no matter what their circumstances. Play is indeed basic and all children will find their own ways of exercising that need whenever they get the chance. The problem is that for some children, the opportunities are very few.

As children have no political voice of their own, their needs are vulnerable and often ignored. In the childhood field, we have not yet managed to present strong enough arguments to convince politicians that children are the most important long-term investment for the future economic health of the community. Somehow it is hard for policymakers to see children as future adults, as workers, leaders, consumers, and

taxpayers. Therefore, the Convention on the Rights of the Child must be the voice for all children.

The Convention on the Rights of the Child

The Convention of the Rights of the Child is a critically legal document that connects all of us who work with or on behalf of children. It covers comprehensively the human and civil rights of all children, everywhere — including the right to play. The Convention was adopted by the United Nations General Assembly on November 20, 1989, and came into force on September 2, 1990 (UNICEF).

As of October, 1992, the latest information on the status of the Convention obtained from the UNICEF Office on Children's Rights, New York, (1-0212-326-7307) was as follows:

- 123 countries of 186 member countries had *ratified* the convention and have thereby had become States Parties to the Convention. They must abide by its conditions and must adhere to a reporting schedule to the UN Human Rights Commission in Geneva.

- 27 additional countries had signed the Convention — i.e., had made a moral commitment to proceed with ratification.

- 36 countries had done nothing. This group includes the USA, *the only Western country that still had taken no action.*

The three main arguments that have been expressed at various times as reasons for inaction of the USA are:

1. The Convention is not a federal matter since the states of the union have laws that cover all of the issues addressed by Convention. *Response:* Many other countries with states and also a strong federal system of government (Canada and Australia in particular) have ratified the Convention. Clearly, in the con-

text of the United Nations, the Convention is intended as a matter for national policy.

2. Abortion is not addressed by the Convention. Since the Convention does not take a stand for or against, the argument is that the Convention is tacitly supports abortion. *Response:* Since even the Vatican has ratified the Convention, this argument seems extremely weak.

3. Capital punishment. The Convention says that no one can be punished for capital crimes committed before the age of eighteen. Several states in the Union have laws that contravene this right, therefore, if the U.S.A. took action on the Convention it would be in contravention with the established law in some states. *Response:* The U.S. government has made no effort to bring the state governors together to urge them to bring their state laws in lie with this basic human right contained in the Convention. It represents as excellent opportunity to rid the nation of the outmoded, barbaric laws that every other Western industrial nation has abolished.

The Right To Play

Article 31 of the Convention, [which the International Association for the Child's Right to Play (IPA) endorses and supports] specifically addresses the child's right to play. It states:

1. Parties recognize the right of the child to rest and leisure, to engage in play and recreational activities appropriate to the age of the child and to participate freely in cultural life and the arts.

2. Parties shall respect and promote the right of the child to participate fully in cultural and artistic life and shall encourage the provision of appropriate and equal opportunities for cultural, artistic, recreational and leisure activity.

According to the United Nations, an unofficial summary of the main provisions of Article 31 can be used under the heading. Leisure, recreation and cultural activities, as follows: *The child has a right to leisure, play, and participation in cultural and artistic activities.*

Interestingly, the word "play" was part of the original draft of the Convention, put there by colleagues in Poland, but later removed. IPA then stepped in to act as an international vigilante to protect the word "play" which some found insignificant.

The right to play is nothing new. It appeared many years ago in the United Nations declaration on the Rights of the Child, now superseded by the more powerful, legally binding Article 31 of the Convention. A related document is the more detailed Declaration on the Child's Right to Play (IPA, 1990). This was drafted originally by IPA in 1977 as a lead to the 1979 International Year of the Child and represents IPA's mission. It reminds us, first, that children are the foundation of the world's future. About play, it says:

Children have played at all times throughout history and in all cultures. Play, along with the basic needs for nutrition, health, shelter, and education, is vital to develop the potential of all children. Play is communication and expression, combining thought and action; it gives satisfaction and a feeling of achievement. Play is instinctive, voluntary, and spontaneous. Play helps children develop physically, mentally, emotionally and socially. Play is a means of learning to live, not a mere passing of time.

Since play is such a powerful, preventative medicine and since Article 31 legally binds the child's right to play, let's look more closely at some ways Article 31 affects society.

The Power of Play

Children do not need permission to play. It is their natural state of being. Children will play, anyway, anywhere in the interstices of the adult world. Without play, a child's personality and full potential as an individual has much less chance of flourishing. For Children living under very stressful conditions — such as family abuse or that most extreme form of mass child abuse, war — it is perhaps their only hope for conserving their humanity. Play is used as a therapeutic technique for helping children recover from horrors that could otherwise become lifetime psychological scars.

War and Peace

One of the most terrible threats to peace and the survival of the planet is the number of places where whole generations of children have grown up without playing. Either political or social violence has made playing virtually impossible or even worse, the children themselves are part of the violence. The tendency towards violence, particularly the commercialized violence manufactured in the United States and exported to the rest of the world, is especially sinister because of the unwillingness of most national governments to control it. In 1988, IPA was appointed as a United Nations Peace Messenger because of its fight against video violence and the production and sale of war toys and its promotion of play as a strategy for pace on the other.

Space for Play

Space is a basic resource that children need in order to play. It is by this measure that we can begin to judge how seriously a community is attending to the needs of its children. In 1979 the IPA sponsored an international survey to see how many countries had either standards or guidelines obligating the developers of family housing to set aside space for children's play (Esbensen, 1974). A follow-up study 10 years later showed virtually no change in the situation (Moore, 1990). At the time of this last count, 18 countries had some form of national guideline and of these, 12 also had a specific standard for children's outdoor space in residential developments. Only one country, Norway, has a broad legal requirement to address children's needs in local municipal planning, and for young people to participate in the development of those plans.

Playing and Learning

To play is to learn -- about oneself and the world we live in. Children who have good quality play experiences have a greater chance of acquiring greater self-esteem and of becoming more productive, responsible members of society. To achieve a competitive role in the global economy, it will also be necessary to have the following essential working skills:
• Creativity, imagination, vision, visual thinking
• Adaptability to ever-changing environments
• Flexibility to adjust (with good humor) to new positions at a moment's notice
• Collaborative group-working, problem-solving skills
These key skills develop in children as they play. They are skills that children learn naturally provided they have access to stimulating play spaces and creative, caring adults who can

greatly extend the impact of play on children's capacity for learning. This is even more true for children with disabilities.

Children with Disabilities

Article 23 of the Convention recognizes the rights of children with disabilities. In summary it states:
> A disabled child has the right to special care, education and training to help him or her enjoy a full and decent life in dignity and achieve the greatest degree of self-reliance and social integration possible.

Congress enacted the Americans with Disabilities Act (ADA) 1990. The result of the collective political effort of many organizations working together, the ADA is a major achievement in the legal support of civil rights of people with disabilities. Even more recently, efforts have been made to ensure that the implementation of the ADA also addresses the access needs of children (Center for Accessible Housing, 1992).

Many design innovations in play settings in both the U.S.A. and Europe have provided more comfortable and equitable opportunities for integration of children with and without disabilities (see Table 1). Usability and the support of independent behavior are the keys to design for integration. Children should feel that they can act independently and have as much control as possible over their environment. Children, like adults, have different levels of ability and need environments that offer different levels of challenge. Each child needs to achieve a satisfying level of independent choice. These are key concepts in the design of spaces for children's play. Diversity and choice, usability and independence together represent the idea of Universal Design. This is the antithesis of the old idea of designing "special places" for "special people" (Moore, Goltsmany & Iacofano, 1992).

Play and Environment

Play is a means that all children use to discover cognitive and sensory stimulation in their environment. It is a means of learning about the natural and social world. The extent to which this is possible depends largely on the design of the physical content and form of the space.

Table 1 is a short, selected international list of play spaces designed to maximize social and environmental interaction in a variety of contexts:

Conclusion

Play is the right of all children. From analyzing the power of play, to playing for peace, playing in adequate spaces, playing for learning, and playing for the integration of all children, play perhaps, in a very fundamental way, represents the deepest level of human meaning. Play is an innate force within each individual and a powerful way for people to learn to live together. As adults, we have a responsibility, as guaranteed to children in Article 31, to create fertile places where play can flourish vigorously.

References

Bengtsson, A., Ed. (1972). *Adventure playgrounds*. New York: Preager.

Brett, A., Moore, R. C., & Provenzo, E. F. (In press). *The complete playground book*. Syracuse, N.Y.: Syracuse University Press.

Esbensen, S. B. (1979). An international inventory and comparative study of legislation and guidelines for children's play spaces in the residential environment. Ottawa, Canada: Canada Mortgage and Housing Corporation.

Hewlett, S. A. (1991). *When the bough breaks: The cost of neglecting our children*. New York: Basic Books. (See p. 45 and related note. The author quotes estimates of the number of homeless people in the U.S. at between 600,000 and three million. Approximately 30 percent of them were estimated to be parts of families consisting of a parent with two or three children. Based on these figures, the lowest estimate of homeless children is therefore 300,000. If this is anywhere near the truth it is a damning indictment of current public policy ... or lack thereof.)

International Play Association. (1990). *Declaration of the child's right to play*. London: I.P.A. Resources.

Michaelis, B. (1979). Adventure playgrounds: A healthy affirmation of the rights of the child. *Journal of the Physical Education and Recreation Association*, 55.

Moore, R. C. (1989). Before and after asphalt: Diversity as an ecological measure of quality in children's outdoor environments. In Block, M. & Pelligrini, T, Eds., *The ecological context of children's play*, p. 203. Norwood, N.J.: Ablex.

Moore, R. C. (1990). *International approaches to planning for children's playspace: Action for play; Planning for the twenty-first century*. London: National Playing Fields Association.

Center for Accessible Housing. (1992). Recommendations for accessibility standards for children's environments; final technical report to the Federal Architectural and Transportation Barriers Compliance Board. N.C.: Author.

Moore, R. C., Goltsman, S. M., & Iacofano, D. S. (1992). *Play for all guidelines: Planning, design, and management of outdoor play settings for all children*, 2nd ed. Berkeley, Calif.: MIG Communications.

Spitzer, K. (1989). The open playground. *PlayRights*, 10(1), 2-7.

UNICEF. Convention on the Rights of the Child briefing kit. New York: Center for Human Rights.

ROBIN C. MOORE is international president of the International Association for the Child's Right to Play and a professor of landscape architecture at North Carolina State University.

Name	Location	Description
Development Center	Cleveland, OH	Educational institution for young children with disabilities, diverse indoor-outdoor environment.
Aldgate Kindergarten Aldgate Elementary School	Adelaide, Australia	Both emphasize vegetation, sand, water, and an ecological approach to learning.
Playspace	Raleigh, NC	Downtown indoor playspace emphasizing dramatic and sensory play.
Playport	Raleigh-Durham International Airport	Dramatic play space for waiting children and parents.
Adventure Playground First Adventure Playground	Emdrup, Copenhagen	Play and building opportunities for children using earth, fire, water, and timber. Now 50 years old. Fascinating to visit.
Numerous	England	Lady Allen of Hurtwood initiated many throughout the UK.
Children's Farms	Netherlands, Germany and England	Variety of styles and programs, but all focus on animals.
Ecological Parks	London	Emphasis on rehabilitation of spoilt inner city and for community education/recreation.
Environmental Yard	California	Adventure play and enivornmental learning action/research project developed on a school site.
The Open Playground	Dusseldorf, Germany	Evolving ecological space, built and used by the whole community

Table 1

Chapter 4
Play and Playscapes: Issues in the 1990s

JOE L. FROST

A decade ago (June, 1983) an International Conference on Play was held at the University of Texas at Austin. Many of the participants and planners of today's American Association for the Child's Right to Play (IPA)* conference were present. At the closing session of that 1983 conference, I reflected about issues on play and the mission of play proponents for the 1980s. Today, I will revisit a few of these issues and reflect on their importance for the 1990s.

Understanding Play

A decade ago I proposed that we should seek to improve our understanding of play by studying the phenomenon, distinguishing it from related variables, and in so doing, illuminate its characteristics and meaning. Toward these ends, students of play have produced many correlational studies, further strengthening the connection between play and development. Others have reflected about play, integrating the growing body of research from various disciplines to form a more unified view. Still others are turning to alternative research methods to probe more deeply into the intricacies of play. Ethnographic, observational, case study methods, and refinements such as grounded theory are among the promising alternatives to traditional experimental methods of research. We are indeed improving our understanding of play, but the generic concept of play is subordinate to a wide range of motives, characteristics, functions and developmental correlates and defies precise definition.

In our search to understand play, we are learning what play is not, overturning such time-honored but misguided tenets as "play is the child's work." That conclusion, emerging from the 1930 White House Conference on Child Health and Protection, unwittingly confessed the confusion about play and work and misguided several generations of professionals and parents. Some of our most prominent scholars — John Dewey (1966), Jean Piaget (1962), Johan Huizinga (1939), L.S. Vygotsky (1978), Mihaly Csikszentmihalyi (1975, 1990) — helped to clarify the play/work distinction (Table 1), explaining that they are distinct but related activities. (Even children know the difference.) Play is a special activity, possessing certain attributes and encompassing certain experiences that distinguish it from work. The quality of the experience sets play apart from non-play. In play, the child is free to enter and free to leave. Our goal for children is that the lucid qualities of play permeate their work. The contrast between play and work is neither conclusive or fixed. Play can be very serious and work can be quite joyful. Subordinating play to external goals (e.g., academic, concrete rewards) or reducing work to mere amusement or aimlessness is neither satistfying nor profitable for children's development. As young children mature through play, their natural tendency and notivation is to follow a developmental trend in play and work, to engage in more complex forms of thought, and to focus increasingly on reality and industry. The absence of a hard-and-fast distinction between play and work allows the extension of joyful, spiritual qualitites of play to the work experience.

This is not to suggest that all activities should be playful or that play should be the dominant activity of young children. Children learn and develop through both work and play and both are appropriate at home and school. To counteract the growing disability of children in industrialized societies to use tools and engage in meaningful, joyful, productive work, the American Association for the Child's Right to Play

(IPA) can promote understanding of the importance of tool-using skills for children and help to reeducate professionals who assist children in learning work roles.

Playground Injuries and Hazards

A decade ago, we were concerned about the rising incidence of children's playground injuries reported through the National Electronic Injury Surveillance System (NEISS) (117,951 in 1974; 167,000 in 1978; almost 200,000 in 1983 (Frost, 1992). This number of injuries continued at an annual 200,000-plus rate for several years and had climbed to about a quarter million annually by 1992. This dramatic increase in reported injuries can perhaps best be explained by the finding of three national surveys of American playgrounds. The first was a survey of American public elementary school play-

grounds (Bruya & Langendorfer, 1988), the second was a survey of American public park playgrounds (Thompson & Bowers, 1989) and the third was a survey of American preschool playgrounds (Wortham & Frost, 1990). Overall, the results from over 700 playgrounds surveyed in most of the 50 states revealed a pattern of poor equipment design, faulty installation, improper surfacing and poor or nonexistent maintenance. Public schools ranked lowest among the three locations (public schools, public parks, preschools) on measures of safety and preschools ranks highest. In general, all three types received very poor scores. Public school playgrounds conformed remarkably well to the hopelessly inadequate 1931 guidelines of the National Recreation Association (1931).

Given the increase in rate of playground injuries over the past two decades and the find-

	Qualities Essential for Play	Qualities of Work
Dewey	Activity as end Employs native tendencies Incidental	End is central Results are foreseen Planned
Piaget	Assimilation End in itself Spontaneous Pleasurable Free of organized structure Free of conflicts	Accommodation External ends Compulsive Utilitarian Ordered Conflicts
Huizinga	Voluntary activity Pretense Free (freedom)	Planned task Real Life Imposed by physical necessity
Vygotsky	Imaginary need fulfillment Play changes and matures	Emphasis on reality Developmental trend from play to work
Csikszentmihalyi	Intrinsic motivation Peak experience Flow experiences Spirit of play	Spirit of play applicable to work but rarely achieved in work

Table 1
Play-work relationships. Adapted from Frost, J. L. (1992). *Play and playscapes*. Albany, N.Y.: Delmar.

ings of the national surveys, a critical issue emerges. Were manufacturers continuing to market hazardous equipment during the 1980s? Was the available equipment consonant with the 1981 United States Consumer Product Safety Commission Guidelines (U.S.C.P.S.C., 1981a, 1981b)? In response to this question, the playground equipment of 24 companies distributing nationwide was analyzed and compared with C.P.S.C. Guidelines (1981a, 1981b) using 1989 catalogs, equipment specifications and first-hand inspections. The initial investigator's analysis (Frost, 1990) was verified in blind analysis by other playground specialists (90% agreement.) The results showed that the equipment of three companies had "no observable violations" and nine companies had "limited violations" or "some violations." Most of these could be readily corrected. Twelve of the companies, or half of these surveyed, offered for sale playground equipment with "extensive violations" or "extreme violations." In general, practically every type of playground equipment manufactured in the United States during this century could still be purchased in 1990 from one or more American companies.

The still-growing array of lawsuits brought by parents of seriously- and fatally-injured children have in macabre fashion captured the attention of most designers, manufacturers, and sponsors of children's playgrounds. This has led, fortunately, to unparalleled interest in safety by preschool and public park administrators and fast food restaurateurs. The notable exception is public schools. Protected by law from tort liability claims and free of any state playground regulations in most states, American public school playgrounds in 1992 are perhaps the worst in the world, hazardous, developmentally sterile, and rooted in unbelievable ignorance about history, research, and values of play. This state of knowledge and resulting lack of commitment is matched by a few manufacturers who continue to cling to archaic design, philosophy, and practice and steadfastly resist change and progress. Such manufacturers are rapidly becoming the exception, for others are creating a rich collection of play materials and equipment for children and are resolute in their efforts to make play environments developmentally challenging and environmentally sensitive, yet fun and safe.

My involvement and first-hand accounts of my peers who are expert witnesses in child injury cases lead me to conclude that an intolerable burden of guilt should be borne by only a few manufacturers whose equipment is responsible — year after year, decade after decade — for thousands of easily preventable injuries. These same manufacturers, repeatedly sued by parents over the decade of the 90's and the subject of formal complaints and action by the United States Consumer Product Safety Commission and the United State Department of Justice, steadfastly deny fault, resist product recall or improvement, and continue to claim that their products meet the C.P.S.C. Safety Guidelines. The scope of the injuries and their ties to a few manufacturers is perhaps best known to those directly involved in litigation for most of the cases are settled out-of-court and are not matters of public record or awareness. Manufacturers not implicated in repeated litigation on defective products and even the sales personnel of implicated companies tend to be uninformed about the scope and nature of playground injuries and resulting litigation tied to the products of the companies most frequently involved. The secrecy and unavailability of information about playground injury litigation settled out of court masks both the extent and nature of injuries and the features of implicated playground equipment. The N.E.I.S.S. data are too general to reveal specific causes of injury or specific features of implicated equipment. To cite one of many available examples, N.E.I.S.S. playground injury data concluded that 300 children were burned on playground equipment during 1988. These data were generally unavailable or overlooked by playground professionals, even in their deliberations to develop national playground safety guidelines and standards, until a plaintiffs' attorney in 1991 produced photographs and incidence data revealing a long-standing pattern of severe burns on bare metal decks and slides. This led to a section on burns in the 1991 C.P.S.C. Guidelines for Public Playground Equipment (U.S.C.P.S.C., 1991).

Despite the current revolution in playground

design and development, due substantially to IPA. members, our goal of improving play spaces for children is more complex than ever. Concerns for safety have resulted in a growing array of safety directives, guidelines, standards, and laws. Many of us have worked with C.P.S.C. for over a decade, collecting and contributing research and participating in deliberations, resulting in C.P.S.C. safety guidelines that are imperfect, yet skillfully and democratically developed. The emerging A.S.T.M. standards expected to be published in late 1993 are being developed in similar fashion and will complement C.P.S.C. guidelines.

Now other groups are distributing competing guidelines and standards. The Consumer Federation of America report (Morrison & Fise, 1992) though commendable in many respects, replicates C.P.S.C. data, introduces contradictory elements, and omits critical factors. The American Health and Pediatrics Association safety guidelines for playgrounds are unbelievably bad — filled with errors and guidelines contradicatory to C.P.S.C. data and acceptable professional practice. Five years ago as president of the American Association for the Child's Right to Play, I followed an IPA resolution by petitioning the C.P.S.C. to revise the 1981 guidelines and provided assistance in helping to ensure broad-based membership on the A.S.T.M. standards committees. IPA encouraged the C.P.S.C./A.S.T.M. process, IPA assisted in the development, and IPA should promote their products — even as we work to improve them. The alternative is confusion among designers, manufacturers and consumers and lengthy, extensive litigation pitting professional against professional and standard against standard.

Research on Play Environments

A decade ago, isolated studies of play environments were beginning to signal differences in the play behavior of children on traditional, limited-function playgrounds and on playgrounds designed for a wide range of play and developmental needs. In general, these studies showed that rich, well-equipped playgrounds broaden and enhance play; that complexity in play materials and equipment solicit complexity and enrich play; that play materials shape play. Now, moving beyond quantitative to qualitative analyses, we confirm those earlier observations and see that the very *quality* of play is influenced by the nature and range of play materials and equipment. Anecdotal and time sampling studies of carefully-planned, extensively-equipped playgrounds by graduate students at the University of Texas (Barbour, 1993; Moore, 1992; Riddell, 1992; Frost & Deacon, 1993) show clear, precise advantages over common, traditional playgrounds:

- More types of social interaction
- Greater frequency of social interaction
- More use of language
- Greater variety of language communications
- More dramatic and construction play
- Higher quality of dramatic play
- Greater variety of play themes
- More object transformations
- More environmental transformations
- Greater duration, persistence and continuity of play and play themes
- Reduced non-occupied and aggressive behavior

The importance of creating opportunities for a range of play is further validated by studies linking play and learning. Recent case studies by my colleagues at the University of Texas (Yeatman and Reifel, 1992) show that children in free, undirected play do learn, they progress through play from a state of ignorance to state of knowing. They learn new information, skills and social rules and they develop internal models that facilitate later learning.

During the past decade, knowledge about the nature of play has expanded rapidly. Concurrently, research into play environments has confirmed many old assumptions and broadened the knowledge base. Many unpublished doctoral dissertations on play and play environments have yet to find their way into professional journals, including over twenty at the University of Texas alone. A sampling of general conclusions from these studies illustrate the nature and scope of findings.

Beginning in infancy, play environments should be matched to children's developmental tendencies (Wagner, 1981; Winter, 1983; Chiang, 1985; Keesee, 1990; Barbour, 1993). Early sensory and exploratory activities of infants and toddlers are quickly supplemented with pretend play and ever-expanding abilities to engage in complex, challenging gross-motor activities. Many play materials and practically all large fixed equipment are quickly "outgrown" when children have extensive daily periods (at least 30 to 60 minutes) of free, active play on well-equipped playgrounds. The outdoor environment, no less than the indoor environment, should be matched to the rapidly developing abilities of children — constantly changing, constantly growing, constantly becoming more complex and challenging. Chronological age, though a useful general guideline, is less meaningful than developmental abilities in matching children to play environments. For example, two-year-olds, when allowed time to explore challenging materials and equipment, develop motor skills at remarkable rates. Existing exercise equipment rapidly loses its effectiveness and must be modified or replaced by more challenging equipment. Multiple play areas featuring many levels of challenge should be considered when planning play environments. Finally, every public playground must now meet the needs of all children - those with extraordinary abilities and those with disabilities.

The features of developmentally appropriate play equipment include complexity, multiple function, novelty, linkage, manipulability, action orientation, and flexibility (Strickland, 1979; Dean, 1981; Jones, 1985; Frost & Campbell, 1985; Moore, 1992; Barbour, 1993; Frost & Deacon, 1993). For infants and toddlers, equipment should integrate sensory, exploratory, and action-oriented devices. These include multiple challenges and levels of complexity at entry and exit points, devices that produce sound (drums, bells, etc.) require manipulation (steering wheels, etc.) and provide gross motor challenge (slides, climbers, etc.). Preschool children's environments must be expanded to provide even greater levels of cognitive, social and motor challenge while adding materials to solicit and enhance make-believe and construction play. Gross-motor equipment is best linked in ways to solicit and support chase games and related make-believe activities that are emerging during the preschool period. Well-planned equipment linkage (arranging equipment to provide many choices within a limited area) also reduces conflicts, bottlenecks, and stand-in-line behavior at points of entry and exit. Consequently, behavior problems are reduced (Strickland, 1979; Keesee, 1990; Moore, 1992).

Gender differences in outdoor play are evident early, become more pronounced with age, and are influenced by adults and available materials and equipment. (Henniger, 1977; Myers, 1981; Winter, 1983; Chiang, 1985; Frost, Horney, Kim, Lin & Yang, 1993). The repetitive motor play (e.g., climbing, pushing, pedaling) of male and female toddlers is similar but there are marked differences in the type of play materials chosen. Boys select action materials (e.g., barrels, balls, crates) and engage in gross-motor activities while girls tend to select domestic materials (e.g., dolls, containers, tea sets) and engage in fine manipulation. The frequency in selecting stationary gross-motor equipment (e.g., overhead bars, climbers, slides) is smiliar for boys and girls but there are strong differences in specific gross-motor equipment selected. In well-equipped playgrounds, preschool boys engage in more cooperative and dramatic play than girls and girls engage in more constructive and functional (exercise or gross-motor) play. These patterns change in the primary grades as boys increasingly turn to organized games and girls engage in functional, dramatic, and constructive play. All of these patterns at all ages are heavily influenced by the type and range of materials equipment and space available, so specific conclusions for all types of playgrounds are not warranted. The support, expectations and dictates of adults also influence gender differences in play as well as the overall play and equipment choices of children at all ages.

The influence of adults on children's play is far greater than generally believed. Training in play leadership, even in limited amounts, leads to significant positive changes in caregiver behavior and child behavior during outdoor play (Vernon, 1976; Wade, 1980; Monroe, 1983; Dempsey, 1985; Frost, Horney, Kim Lin, & Yang, 1993) In general, teachers are uninformed about the play preferences of children (Monroe, 1983). As few as four to five hours in play leadership training results in more positive interaction between adults and children, correlating positively with the provision of better-equipped playgrounds and encouragement of greater variety of play roles and themes. The need for play leadership training on gender stereotyping for teacher and caretakers is seen in their expectations for gender-related play, provision of materials for play, and their interactions with children during play. For example, primary-school teachers support highly competitive organized games (soccer, basketball, etc.,) for boys and accept onlooker activity and contrived, stereotypical role play and functional play for girls in the same group. Play leadership training also assists adults in understanding the effects of extensive television-viewing on children's play and development. Television adversely affects play themes and reduces time available for more productive and beneficial activities (Guddemi, 1985). Finally, play leadership training can help adults overcome established misconceptions about the nature and value of play. For example, common practice in equipping playgrounds and encouraging play suggest that upon entry to primary school, children have outgrown their inclination and need for dramatic play materials. Children continue their zest for dramatic and construction play through the primary grades (Jackson, 1990) and in well-equipped playgrounds primary-age children, especially boys, engage in competitive, organized games but engage in a greater variety of play that do children in sterile playgrounds equipped exclusively with limited-function fixed equipment.

The developmentally appropriate playground is much more than a collection of single or limited function pieces of heavy apparatus. A range of loose, portable materials are needed to promote the range of play activities that are natural for any given age group (Henniger, 1977; Barbour, 1993; Frost & Deacon, 1993). Loose, portable materials are the major content of preschooler's play. These include raw materials (e.g., tools, blocks), a range of art, gardening, nature-related, and pet supplies, and a range of both theme-specific (e.g., dolls, cars) and nontheme-specific items (e.g., building blocks). Portable materials must be readily accessible from storage facilities located on the playground and near sand and water areas, play houses, construction areas, and other areas and equipment that depend on loose

materials for generalization of play roles, themes and constructions.

Creating Magical Playscapes

Research on play and play environments is increasingly affecting the quality of children's play opportunities and play materials, yet tradition and societal changes conspire toward sterile, uninspired, high-tech playgrounds designed to appeal to adult tastes and to entertain children. The growing array of "pay-for-play" places such as the glittery, violence-centered video-games of Las Vegas' Circus-Circus playscapes illustrate the most extreme extravagances of a generation bent on self-indulgence. The quick-fix of computer games, TV, and commercial playscapes now substitute for quality family time and creative, magical play places that enhance development rather than merely entertain. Talbot and Frost (1989) proposed qualities of magical playscapes for children — playscapes that transcend the usual and become vibrant, enchanting, places.

Changing of Scale: Three scales — miniature, child-sized, and colossal — extend children's capacities and sense of personal power (e.g., models, tiny animals, child-sized trains, dinosaurs).

The Suggestions of Other Beings: Children gain a sense of power by hearing stories about small versions of themselves — brownies, pixies, fairies — and a sense of magic is felt in a place inhabited by them (e.g., Santa's workshop, cozy garden setting for reading stories).

Realness: Children prefer the real to the sham. The degree of detail, the link to known entities, the functional qualities all endow the user with special capabilities (e.g., real fire engines, tools).

Archetypal Images: Childhood values, myths, fairy tales, and their symbolic play (e.g., stars, moon, trees).

Sense of "Placeness": Magical places have an ambiance that sets them apart from the everyday world (e.g., amphitheater, garden, fireplace).

Open-endedness: Objects with open-ended functions lend themselves to many uses. Such objects are open to many uses and give children the power to say what they will be or do (e.g., cardboard boxes, building blocks).

Nature and the Elements: The playscape opens up

possibilities to interact with nature and its elements — earth, air, fire, and water. Nature offers levels of meaning far beyond the artificial or manufactured (e.g., gardens, orchards, groves, streams).

Line Quality and Shape: Arches, curves, cloud shapes, hanging shapes, and topsy-turvy shapes enhance the line quality of playscapes (e.g., arched doorways, mobiles, rolling hills).

Sensuality: Places that engage the senses — rich color, fragrances, pleasant sounds, engaging textures, varied light qualities - heighten and sustain enchantment and meaning of any experience (e.g., blooming flowers, chimes, sensory walks).

Layering: Objects or views that are "framed" by layers of foreground materials heighten sense of depth and feeling of richness and increase the degree of complexity (e.g., vegetation, walls, hills).

Novelty: Rarity, unusualness, unpredicatability, and incongruity expand children's perceptions of the world and lend a sense of specialness (e.g., totem poles, tire animals, pipe telephone systems).

Mystery: Nooks, crannies, and enchanted forests offer surprise and discovery.

Brilliance: Young children are delighted with sparkling, gleaming, glittering surfaces. Playyards can contain mesmeric qualities of such things (e.g., mirrors, tile, light reflecting prisms).

Juxtaposition of Opposites: A certain epic quality, a largeness of purpose, is suggested when opposites are at play with each other (e.g., hard/soft surfaces, rounded/straight lines, sunlight/shadow, contrasting and complimentary colors).

Richness and Abundance: Very little can be created in a vacuum. Children need an environment rich in possibilities with no sense of scarcity (e.g., storage, building supplies and tools, vegetation, events).

Connection with Other Times, Other Places: Age and history bestow a magical aura. Age implies an unknown quality that leads to speculation and expanding imagination (e.g., preserving old trees on the playground, old building materials, Chinese sculptures).

"Is-ness": Not everything in the playyard needs to be functional. Add something with no other purpose than to express a meaning beyond utility and reasoning (e.g., a flower garden, a tree hanging, a graphic design).

Loose Parts and Simple Tools: Add materials that allow the child to transform mere junk into personal creations and wonderlands (e.g., tools, scrap materials).

The Illusion of Risk: Peak experiences during moments of apparent risk place the mind in a state of alertness, resourcefulness, and expectancy. Mastering perceived threats results in growth spurts and affirmations of personal power (e.g., hillside slides, guided use of fire, wilderness adventure hikes).

Doing Nothing: Substitute recess, free time, leisure, and fun for tightly structured lessons, practices, schedules, and television. Give kids time for messing around with valued friends in enchanting places.

Conclusion

Given the rapidly accumulating evidence of the importance of play in learning and development, it is an affront to play scholars and a violation of the basic rights of children that time for free play (recess) should be abandoned or replaced by formal, structured activites. Sutton-Smith (1990) observed even less variety on today's school playgrounds and greater supervision and structure than on those of their own childhood. Free play on the schoolyard is a cultural and social event of long endurance and great importance. American children, indeed all children, should have certain inalienable rights to free association, free speech, periodic rest periods, and festival occasions such as those offered in traditional recess. One of the fundamental goals of the IPA is to preserve the right to free play for all children.

A little-known fact is that major health hazards for American children no longer stem from disease but from accidental injuries and unintentional and intentional injuries. Further, it is still not widely understood or acknowledged that childhood accidents are preventable. *Accidental injury is not a natural or inevitable consequence of growing up,* and we should no longer accept or tolerate the existence of life-threatening hazards in children's play environments.

IPA can identify and recognize publicly the exceptional efforts by many designers, engineers, architects, child development professionals, and manufacturers who spare no effort in ensuring safely and playability of playgrounds. I.P.A. also can help to forge research partnerships between professionals to ensure that playground equipment is subjected to scientific scrutiny in both laboratory and field contexts. I express appreciation to BigToys for the research partnership they have initiated with University of Texas researchers and to Grounds for Play, Iron Mountain Forge and Kompan for their continuing support for field research and the work of I.P.A.

Finally, IPA cannot be content with evolution from antiquated, hazardous, limited-function playgrounds to contemporary high-tech, "cookie cutter" (Beckwith, 1991) playgrounds. The notion that either constitutes an acceptable playscape is untenable and contrary to both experience and research. In these final years before the 21st century, the best created playscapes for children must capture and preserve the character and intent of our most innovative, dedicated people:

The community spirit stimulated by Paul Hogan and Robert Leathers.

The ambiance of nature and raw materials valued by Robin Moore and Roger Hart.

The sensitivity to child differences and disabilities expressed in the work of Lady Allen of Hurtwood and Susan Goltsman.

The qualities of aesthetics — of beauty — proposed by Anita Olds.

The lucid flow and freedom of Mihaly Csikszentmihalyi and Johan Huizinga.

The concern for culture, relativity, and recess defended by Brian Sutton-Smith.

The playscapes of the 21st century must integrate nature and technology so that children come to know through work and through play the fragility of the ecosystem on which we depend — so that they can explore nature and can create with their own hands — so they can capture and recapture the magical, mysterious qualities of childhood that so many adults seem to have forgotten.

References

Barbour, A. (1993). Physical competence and peer relations: Case studies of eight first-graders. Unpublished doctoral dissertation, The University of Texas at Austin.

Beckwith, J. (1991). *No more cookie cutter playgrounds*. Forestville, Calif.: Beckwith Associates, Ltd.

Bell, M. J. (1989). Peer leadership and its influence on the outdoor activities of preschool play groups. Unpublished doctoral dissertation, The University of Texas at Austin.

Bruya, L. D. & Langendorfer, S. J. (Eds.). (1988). *Where our children play: Elementary school playground equipment*. Reston, Va.: American Alliance for Health, Physical Education, Recreation and Dance.

Campbell, S.D. & Frost, J. L. (1985). The effects of playground type on the cognitive and social play behaviors of grade two children. In J.L. Frost & S. Sunderlin (Eds.), *When children play*. Wheaton, Md.: Association for Childhood Education International.

Chiang, L. (1985). Developmental differences in children's use of play materials. Unpublished doctoral dissertation, The University of Texas at Austin.

Csikszentmihalyi, M. (1975). *Beyond boredom and anxiety: The experience of play in work and games*. San Francisco: Jossey-Bass.

Csikszentmihalyi, M. (1990). *Flow: The psychology of optimal experience*. New York: Harper & Row.

Dean, D. G. (1981). Motor behaviors of kindergartners during physical education and free play. Unpublished doctoral dissertation, The University of Texas at Austin.

Dempsey, J. D. (1980). Relationships between questioning and dramatic play of preschool children. Unpublished master's thesis, The University of Texas at Austin.

Dempsey, J. D. (1985). The effects of training in play in cognitive development in preschool children. Unpublished doctoral dissertation, The University of Texas at Austin.

Dewey, J. (1966). *Democracy and education*. New York: The Free Press.

Frost, J. L. (1990). Playground equipment catalogs: Can they be trusted? *Texas Child Care Quarterly, 14*, 3-12.

Frost, J. L. (1992). *Play and playscapes.* Albany, N.Y.: Delmar.

Frost, J. L. & Campbell, S. D. (1985). Equipment choices of primary-age children on conventional and creative playgrounds. In J. L. Frost and S. Sunderlin (Eds.), *When children play.* Wheaton, Md.: Association for Childhood Education International.

Frost, J. L. & Deacon, D. (1993). Influences of environment on play behaviors of primary school children. Unpublished research paper, The University of Texas at Austin.

Frost, J. L., Horney, J., Kim, H., Lin, S., & Yang, S. (1993). Play behavior and equipment choices of third grade children on contrasting playgrounds. Unpublished research paper, The University of Texas at Austin.

Guddemi, M. (1985). The effects of television on children's play themes. Unpublished doctoral dissertation, The University of Texas at Austin.

Henniger, M. L. (1977). Free play behaviors of nursery school children in an indoor and outdoor environment. Unpublished doctoral dissertation, The University of Texas at Austin.

Huizinga, J. (1950). *Homo ludens.* Boston: Beacon Press. (Originally published 1939.)

Jackson, R. S. (1990). The gender stereotyped nature of Christmas gifts for first-, third-, and fifth-grade children: A comparison of children's wish lists and parent inventories. Unpublished doctoral dissertation, The University of Texas at Austin.

Jones, L. M. (1985). Sociodramatic play and problem solving in young children. Unpublished doctoral dissertation, The University of Texas at Austin.

Keesee, L. H. (1990). A comparison of outdoor play environments for toddlers. Unpublished doctoral dissertation, The University of Texas at Austin.

Littleton, D. (1991). Influence of play settings on preschool children's music and play behaviors. Unpublished doctoral dissertation, The University of Texas at Austin.

Monroe, M. L. (1983). Evaluation of day care playgrounds in Texas. Unpublished doctoral dissertation, The University of Texas at Austin.

Moore, M. R. (1992). An analysis of outdoor play environments and play behaviors. Unpublished doctoral dissertation, The University of Texas at Austin.

Morrison, M. L. & Fise, M. E. (1992). *Report and model law on public play equipment and areas.* Washington, D.C.: Consumer Federation of America.

Myers, J. B. (1981). Children's perceived vs. actual choices of playground equipment as perceived by themselves and their teachers. Unpublished doctoral dissertation, The University of Texas at Austin.

National Recreation Association. (1931). Report of Committee on Standards in Playground Apparatus (Bulletin No. 2170). New York: The Association.

Piaget, J. (1962). Play, dreams, and imitation in childhood. New York: W. W. Norton.

Riddell, C. J. (1992). The effects of contrasting playgrounds on the play behaviors of kindergarten children. Unpublished master's thesis, The University of Texas at Austin.

Strickland, E. V. (1979). Free play behaviors and equipment choices of third grade children in contrasting play environments. Unpublished doctoral dissertation, The University of Texas at Austin.

Sutton-Smith, B. (1990). School playground as festival. *Children's Environments Quarterly, 7,* 3-7.

Talbot, J. & Frost, J. L. (1989). Magical playscapes. *Childhood Education, 66,* 11-19.

Thompson, D. & Bowers, L. (Eds.). (1989). *Where our children play: Community park playground equipment.* Reston, Va.: American Alliance for Health, Physical Education, Recreation and Dance.

U.S. Consumer Product Safety Commission. (1981a). *A handbook for public playground safety.* Vol. I: General guidelines for new and existing playgrounds. Washington, D.C.: U.S. Government Printing Office.

U.S. Consumer Product Safety Commission. (1981b). *A handbook for public playground safety.* Vol. II: Technical guidelines for equipment and surfacing. Washington, D.C.: U.S. Government Printing Office.

U.S. Consumer Product Safety Commission. (1991). *Safety guidelines for public playground equipment*. Washington, D.C.: U.S. Government Printing Office.

Vernon, E. A. (1976). <u>A survey of preprimary and primary outdoor learning centers/playgrounds in Texas public schools</u>. Unpublished doctoral dissertation, The University of Texas at Austin.

Vygotsky, L. S. (1978). *Mind in society: The development of higher psychological processes*. Cambridge, Mass.: Harvard University Press.

Wade, C. (1980). Effects of teacher training on teachers and children in playground settings. Unpublished doctoral dissertation, The University of Texas at Austin.

Wagner, B. S. (1981). Assessment of children birth through three years through observation of play behaviors. Unpublished doctoral dissertation, The University of Texas at Austin.

Winter, S. M. (1983). Toddler play behaviors and equipment choices in an outdoor playground. Unpublished doctoral dissertation, The University of Texas at Austin.

Wortham, S. C. & Frost, J. L. (1990). Playgrounds for young children: National survey and perspectives. Reston, Va.: American Alliance for Health, Physical Education, Recreation and Dance.

Yeatman, J. & Reifel, S. (1992). Sibling play and learning. *Play and Culture, 5,* 141-148.

JOE L. FROST, ED.D., is Parker Centennial Professor of early childhood education at The University of Texas at Austin. He is the author of *Play and Playscapes* (Delmar, 1991) and also the author, co-author, editor, or co-editor of more than 100 books, reports, monographs, and articles in early childhood education.

*IPA refers to the original name of the organization, International Playground Association.
*Adapted from Talbot, J. and Frost, J. L. (1989). Magical playscapes. *Childhood Education, 66,* 11-19.

Part II
Play: The Perfect Medicine for Stress

Children are often subject to the same conditions for stress as adults. But, unlike adults, children don't usually have a grasp of the situation nor the defense mechanisms in place to deal with perceptions and realities. The papers in this section look at children with special needs and the role of play as a therapeutic agent.

The number and types of stressors affecting children in our society today are clearly increasing. In their paper, **Fite** and **Beck** zero in on the need to help children develop healthy outlets for stress and life-long coping skills. This may be one of the most important responsibilities that adults have. Listening to children, noticing verbal and nonverbal clues to children's feelings, and supporting their natural inclinations to explore and learn about the world through play are noted as essential for helping children cope. Play is seen by the authors as an excellent context in which children can build a positive self-concept and develop coping strategies to alleviate stress. Fite and Beck provide some excellent examples of play activities which can help children handle stress.

Jessee, Love, and **Derouin** also look at the therapeutic nature of play, but from the point of view of hospital needs. Illness and hospitalization constitute major stressors to a child's development and are likely to produce drastic changes in normal life-style and behaviors. The authors emphasize the importance of play in the lives of children who are hospitalized, even for short periods of time, and feel that health care providers can facilitate play in a variety of ways. Four distinct functions of play in the hospital are identified as well as two broad forms of play used within this setting: developmental play and medical play. Medical play can promote a multitude of therapeutic functions. The authors provide a number of fine play examples that can help children act out and gain emotional control

over frightening and unfamiliar hospital experiences.

The importance of play to the child in the health care setting is also the subject of **Vogel's** paper. The sheer size and scope of the modern medical center can be overwhelming, according to Vogel, and put the child at risk for some kind of emotional distress. Providing for age-appropriate play can do a lot to relieve the stress and anxieties that frequently accompany health care visits. Seeing play materials and spaces designed for play sends a clear message to both child and parent that the child's need to play is taken seriously. The author also sees the health care staff benefiting. By observing children indulged in play, staff can more accurately assess, diagnose and gain insight into a child's thoughts and feelings. The paper emphasizes that staff, parents and siblings make an important team when planning for a child's play needs in the health care setting, and that well-planned play activities can make the transition from hospital to home or to another hospital smoother and less overwhelming.

In 1990 a community-based program for families of young children with developmental disabilities was initiated in Oklahoma. Known as the Chickasha Project, the program was designed with a threefold purpose: to develop a demonstration model which rural communities could replicate; to publish and disseminate a handbook based on the model and to offer technical assistance to other communities wanting to implement a similar model. **O'Bar** and **Johnsen** provide insight into the role of the parent and family, community volunteers, state and federal support agencies, and play. They discuss the selection of toys, games, or materials for play with regard to the specific needs of the individual children participating in respite program activities.

Chapter 5
Using Play to Alleviate Stress in Young Children

KATHLEEN FITE
SHIRLEY S. BECK

None of us is a stranger to stress. Adults must cope with such stressors as problems at work, lack of money, lack of time, illness, and family conflicts. Stress is the body's physical and mental response to stressors (Morrison, 1988). Over time, and in some cases through repeated efforts, adults develop coping skills. We may use positive outlets such as running, reading, and gardening or not-so-positive ones such as overeating, smoking, and drinking.

Stress manifests itself in all of us. We may feel anxious, frustrated, or angry. We may even become physically ill. On the other hand, we might become happy and excited, even euphoric over a situation. Regardless of the emotional direction, there are also physical changes such as a change in heart rate or muscle tension (Essa, 1992).

Many of the same stressors affect young children. The problem is that children have not had the practice we have had in dealing with stressors and so they have few coping strategies. In many cases, stress is just as intense for children as it is for adults. In fact, it may seem even more unbearable to them because they are not able to put time, consequences, and outcomes into their proper perspective. We need to help them develop healthy outlets for stress and life-long coping skills. We also need to remember that stress is not always bad ... it can have positive, motivating manifestations.

Common Stressors for Children

Stressors for children are categorized as internal or external (Morrison, 1988). *Internal stressors* factors include learning disabilities, physical disabilities, and the child's perceptions of herself and of other significant persons in her life. Regardless of the ploys adults use, a child knows when she is the poorest performer in the group or when he is always the last one chosen to play with his peers. The child who has internalized negative feelings about her selfworth and a sense of rejection from the important adults around her will likely be a stressed child.

External stressors for children include social, emotional, mental, environmental, and physical factors. Poor parenting skills, illness, neglect, fear, inappropriate demands, abuse, violence, separation anxiety, medical treatment, poverty, rejection, and lack of rest are common external stressors.

Children are unable to control or alleviate most of the stressors which affect them. This feeling of helplessness and victimization adds to the child's stress.

How Children React to Stress

Children react to stress in physical, mental or emotional, and social ways much as adults do. For example, a child may overeat or suffer minor illnesses such as a rash, upset stomach, diarrhea, or nail biting. He may withdraw, become aggressive, overly anxious, or hyperactive. Children respond to stressors by developing coping strategies (Morrison, 1988). When searching for a coping strategy, children may select an adaptive or maladaptive approach. Positive action might be finding a substitute activity or a compromise. Negative action might be to throw a tantrum, cry, or become aggressive. How the child reacts depends on his personal experiences and resources at the moment (Essa, 1992). Responses vary between children and for each child depending on the situation. The child might respond differently to the same stress at different times or under different conditions. A major stressor in one child's life may be a minor event to another child. For example, adults may deem a child's action inappropriate when he has a physical or emotional outburst after another child grabs a toy from him, but this event may be the "straw that broke the camel's back" and indicate the child is suffering a high level of stress from other factors.

We may feel uncomfortable and perhaps even helpless when assisting children who are "stressed out." Our reactions, unfortunately, may trigger even more overt behavior. If we are frightened or upset over an action, the child will usually be aware of it and this will add to his anxiety. We must remember that our consistent and calm responses give the children security; if we overreact to upsets, we will probably make the situation worse. On the other hand, ignoring or denying the child's feelings will not remove the stressor or help the child learn to cope.

Listen to the Child

The basis for developing effective coping strategies by children is the acceptance and caring he finds in his teacher or caregiver. Perhaps one of the best ways to show a child that you care is to listen to him. Give him plenty of opportunities to talk about his feelings. When you respond, take time to describe your understanding of the child's feelings before saying anything else. Keep your statements short and uncomplicated. Instead of simply saying that the child seems angry or mad, go on in a more positive tone, perhaps suggesting that he looks like he wishes he had not just acted in a particular way (Hendrick, 1990).

Children need to discover and practice effective coping strategies. Teachers and caregivers have a unique opportunity to help them do this. First, provide many opportunities for the child to build self-concept and self-esteem. This helps him become more resilient. Helping him understand the reasons why some coping strategies are positive and others are negative can assist him in developing an internal conscience which, in turn, will enable him cope with future stressful situations (Essa, 1992). You can accomplish both of these goals while you support the child's natural inclinations to explore and learn about his world through play.

The child needs the adults in her life to be honest about feelings. Adults can add stress by attempting to distract the child or to redirect and deny what she is feeling. Instead of ignoring stress that is building in a young child, adults can demonstrate acceptable "playing out" coping strategies. But the adult must first *notice* verbal and non-verbal clues to the child's feelings.

Play Activities Which Can Help Children Handle Stress

Play is an excellent context in which to build a positive self-concept and to practice positive ways of coping with stress. Here are examples of play opportunities which can help children cope with stress:

Pillows

Provide a pile of pillows somewhere in the classroom. Use sturdy pillows that can take the punishment of pinching, punching, rolling over, and generally mauling. Set limits so that children do not use the pillows to hit other children or objects. One teacher has among her pillows several with faces which regularly have eyes poked, ears and hair pulled, and so forth. The reading center, where a child can be alone for a while to sort through a conflict situation, may be a good place for pillows.

Prop Boxes

Sociodramatic play allows the child to work through possible solutions to problems she is having in personal relationships. Often a new way to behave occurs to a child when a playmate demonstrates strategies the child has not thought of herself. A variety of prop boxes containing relevant items provides children with opportunities to deal with fears related to medical treatment, anger and frustration generated in family conflicts, and other stresses common in their lives. A prop box with a family theme, for example, should include items of clothing that reflect different genders and ages to facilitate playing out family roles. A child who feels unsuccessful and frustrated in dealing with an authoritarian father or an impatient mother may recognize other ways to relate to this parent when a peer counters the usual parent behavior with a different reaction. Stressed children may choose to play the "problem" role in sociodramatic play. We have all had the experience of hearing our own words repeated to dolls, teddy bears, or other children, complete with the exact tone of voice. Perhaps the child, by assuming that role, is attempting to understand that person. Whatever the reason, sociodramatic play with the aid of prop boxes can help a child learn new ways to react from his peers who are not so emotionally bound to the situation.

Housekeeping Center
The housekeeping center can be the setting where a child plays out her perceptions of what is occuring in her family. Remember that what you see reflects the child's perceptions and may not be what has actually happened. For example, the child may believe that her mother takes frequent out-of-town trips because she doesn't love the child, when in fact the mother is taking necessary business trips. The girl may enact her false impression ("Mommy is going away now because she doesn't love you.") at play in the housekeeping center, providing the observant caregiver a clue about other behavior.

A wide variety of dolls (mommy, daddy, brother, sister, baby, grandparents, doctor, dentist, teacher, police officer, "bad man," etc.) encourages children to play out fear, rage, frustration, and jealousy which they may feel. How the teacher or caregiver reacts to the child's expressions of fear or other feelings is critical to alleviating the child's expressions of fear or other feelings. In simple terms, it is okay to feel; what one does as a result of the feeling may be acceptable or unacceptable. The teacher or caregiver can model or suggest appropriate coping strategies if the child appears stymied. However, experienced play therapists often find that children usually have ideas for solutions once they recognize the feelings.

To return to our hypothetical example, the teacher who observes the little girl telling a doll "Mommy is leaving because she doesn't love you" might say, "Gosh, that little girl must feel really sad and scared! What can she do?" The child might reply, "She ought to tell her mother that she's mean!" If not, the teacher could enact that exchange herself, using the doll. Afterwards, the teacher could encourage the little girl to talk to her own mother about her fears. The teacher would also need to report this incident to the parent.

Clay, Water, Mud, and Sand Play
The sensory elements of clay, water, mud, and sand appeal children and allow them to dig, pound, smash, squeeze, rip, and tear in acceptable ways. (Many adults swim or garden to find the same kind of relief from stress.) Unfortunately, teachers and caregivers often restrict children's play in clay, water, mud, or sand. Of course, throwing sand and eating mud or similar activities must be limited. But most of these restrictions are related to getting dirty. How to manage getting dirty is the adult's responsibility. A British teacher filled a child's wading pool with water and dirt and then allowed children dressed in their swim suits to wallow and slide. After each child had a turn, they all trooped off to the showers. No one was concerned with getting dirty, including the teacher who was also dressed in her swim suit! Although one would not plan this activity often, the novelty of being allowed to get caked with mud without the usual recriminations had a profound effect on the children's spirits.

Puppets
Playing with puppets is an especially beneficial way to deal with strong feelings. Attention is focused on the puppet, not the puppeteer. It is safe for the child to display through the puppet what she is hesitant to play or act out in other situations, much less deal with directly in real life. As in sociodramatic play, the child can explore alternative solutions to problems, attempt to understand the behavior of others, or express fully the emotions which are causing stress.

Provide a wide variety of puppets for children to use, including animal and people puppets. Children may play out a stressful situation with animal puppets before they progress to the point of playing it out with people puppets. Role reversals are common in puppet play as they are in sociodramatic play. We can speculate about their reasons for starting with animals but the effect is what we want.

Conclusion

These are examples of how play can be used to counter stress. Almost any play activity can provide opportunities for expressing mental and physical responses to stress. Play is a critical outlet because young children do not have the vocabulary to fully express their feelings.

The stressors affecting children in our society are increasing. Children are further stressed by being unable to express or release their feelings about those stressors. The relief of stress has become one of our most important responsibilities related to children's well being. Play, the child's means of exploring and learning, is a natural choice for alleviating stress in children. When provided in an accepting environment by knowledgeable adults, the therapeutic value of play can be great.

References

Essa, Eva. (1992). *Introduction to early childhood education*. Albany, New York: Delmar Publishing.

Hendrick, Joanne. (1990). *Total learning: Developmental curriculum for the young child*. New York: Merrill Pulbishing.

Hughes, Fergus P. (1991). *Children, Play, and Development*. Needham Heights, Massachusetts: Allyn and Bacon.

Morrison, George S. (1988). *Education and Development of Infants, Toddlers, Preschoolers*. Glenview, Illinois: Scott, Foresman and Co.

KATHLEEN FITE is a professor in the Department of Curriculum and Instruction at Southwest Texas State Univeristy. She has taught, researched, written, and presented in the area of early childhood education for more than 20 years. SHIRLEY S. BECK, an assistant professor, in the Department of Curriculum and Instruction at Southwest Texas State University, has used play therapy as a counseling strategy with young children in public schools.

Chapter 6
Medical Play

PEGGY O. JESSEE
JANE LOVE
DESIREE DEROUIN

Health care providers must continually meet the many needs of their pediatric patients in informed and creative ways. Often nurses, physicians, child life specialists, and others are asked to make professional judgments about a hospitalized child's compliance with medical procedures, adjustment to the hospital environment, degree of pain, and level of psychosocial functioning. In addition, comforting children and alleviating stress are a major concern for all professionals who work with children.

Children play in part to cope with negative stresses. Their play can be a useful tool in diagnosis (Betz & Poster, 1984; Bolig, 1984; Brazelton, 1976; Kleinberg, 1987). Yet health care providers seldom initiate therapeutic play with children in hospitals. Most providers lack the knowledge to effectively help a pediatric patient "play" for therapeutic purposes. Training programs rarely address the subject. Why then, is play a vital tool for comforting children and alleviating pain and stress?

While most adults recognize the importance of play in children's lives, they rarely consider that it follows a sequence similar to the processes of cognitive, social, physical, and emotional growth. Play is necessary for the well-being of the child whether he is sick or well.

Illness and hospitalization constitute major stressors to a child's development and are likely to produce drastic changes in normal life-styles and behaviors (Bergen, Gaynard, & Hausslein, 1987; King & Ziegler, 1981; Newman & Lind, 1980; Oremland, 1988; Thompson & Stanford, 1981). Children's play and other expressive behaviors reveal efforts on their part to master the anxieties of normal development and to relieve the stress of critical emotional experiences (Oremland, 1988). Many methods to ameliorate the psychological trauma of hospitalization and medical procedures for children have been tried, yet, the provision of play programs has consistently been one of the major interventions hospitals have implemented to help children better cope with pain, separation, and loss of control. In the hospital, play supports the cognitive task of understanding a new and strange environment and the emotional task of reconciling fears and lack of control to proceed (Elkins & Roberts, 1983; Rodin, 1983). Play is children's fundamental way of communicating; it allows for self-discovery; it offers reassurance against fear and anxiety; it increases self-esteem through achievement and mastery; and for the pediatric patient, it can reduce time spent in the hospital environment (D'Antonio, 1984; Hall & Cleary, 1988; Thompson & Stanford, 1981). Play facilitates a therapeutic interaction between the heath-care professional and the patient. All of these advantages make play a valuable resource in the treatment of the pediatric patient.

Since play is so important in the lives of children and the absence of play can severely handicap normal growth and development, children who are hospitalized, even for short of time, should have many opportunities to play (Thompson & Stanford, 1981). Health care providers can facilitate play in a variety of ways in the health care setting so that it becomes part of the holistic care of pediatric patients of all ages. However, play in the hospital may be different than normal play and can be more difficult to achieve.

Functions of play in the hospital

Four distinct functions of play in the hospital have been identified:

1. to prepare for medical procedures
2. to enhance communication
3. to master developmental skills, and
4. to cope with negative emotions and stress (Thompson & Stanford, 1981).

These functions have one common thread; that is, in play children learn to deal with cognitively- and emotionally-overwhelming experiences by recreating them in their minds and playing them out in acceptable ways. These factors are pulled together in two broad forms of play used in hospital settings: developmental play and medical play (Bergen, Gaynard, & Hausslein, 1987).

Developmental Play

Developmentally appropriate play meets the child's developmental needs, provides for peer interaction, and offers opportunities to replicate the normal, everyday world of the child. Children in the hospital are usually experiencing an extreme loss of control due to disease or injury. This is compounded by loss of their normal environment. Loss of control can damage children's self-esteem; therefore, providing meaningful play experiences that allow some measure of control by the child becomes doubly important.

To accomplish this, caregivers must create an environment that is safe and secure, that is available at different times throughout the day, and that provides opportunities for decision-making and motor, social, and skill development through age-appropriate activities. The environment should include various materials (e.g., puzzles, blocks, clay, paints, and books) in adequate amounts and provide ready access to toys and materials for children restricted by bulky equipment, such as wheelchairs or by handicapping conditions. Ideally, there also should be several open play spaces that invite diverse kinds of spontaneous play (Vessey & Mahon, 1990).

Medical Play

Medical play, on the other hand, is especially tailored to meet the needs of the hospitalized child. The common characteristics are the use of mock or actual medical equipment and the focus on medical and hospital themes (Gold-

berger, 1984; Petrillo & Sanger, 1980). Medical play can help a child integrate hospital experiences into a more manageable psychological form. It also can actually prepare children for impending medical procedures. By using medical equipment with dolls, puppets, or stuffed animals, children may act out and gain some emotional control over frightening and unfamiliar hospital experiences. Health care providers can use medical play activities to detect and correct misconceptions about medical procedures and to identify unrealistic fears and fantasies (Thompson & Sanford, 1981).

Preadmission tours to the hospital are one kind of medical play experience that serves as a general preparation, introducing pediatric patients to the hospital, allowing them to explore medical equipment, and engaging them in dramatic medical play. Medical play is also used to educate and prepare pediatric patients of all ages for specific procedures. In such play, mock medical procedures should always be carried out on dolls or puppets, rather than the child, to keep the experience as non-threatening as possible. As an adult explains the new procedure to a child, he can use a doll or puppet to demonstrate how the equipment will be used and how the experience may feel to the child (Bergen, Gaynard, & Hausslein, 1987). In this way, medical play can be a diagnostic and educational tool for the health care provider as well as a method of self-expression and mastery for the child (Azarnoff, 1974; Chan, 1980).

In this more directed form of medical play, the *adult* plans which aspects of the experience will be the focus of the planned activity. With some flexibility, the adult sets the pace and controls the content and the process of the play situation. The more the adult controls the activity, the more likely it is that the child will be forced to confront anxiety-arousing issues without psychological resolution (McCue, 1988).

In an alternative approach to medical play, the child identifies the focus of the play activity, sets the pace, and directs the content and process of the play. Play is less purposeful and goal-oriented and more idiosyncratic and process-oriented, supporting the therapeutic benefits of the play (Bolig, 1990). When the child controls the play, she can proceed with psychological integration a little at a time rather than attempting to rush the process and failing when the task becomes overwhelming.

Summary

As health care costs escalate, medical technology advances, and health delivery systems change, the roles of pediatric health care providers are expanding. Children who survive devastating and chronic conditions have complex psychological needs, as do their families. Children's medical conditions that require long-term hospitalization rather than home care will become more intense and the level of knowledge and involvement in psychosocial care also will need to increase. Thus, training programs for pediatric health care providers should incorporate a developmentally appropriate, culturally sensitive, and family-centered approach, using clinical experiences and professional role models (Association for the Care of Childrens' Health, 1989). The result should be pediatric health-care providers who are competent in a much wider range of medical, technological and psychosocial issues than has been necessary in the past. In the hospitals of the next decade, professionals will need to know how to play.

References

Association for the Care of Children's Health. (1989). *Psychosocial guidelines for pediatric care in hospitals*. Bethesda, Md.: Author.

Azarnoff, P. (1974). Mediating the trauma of serious illness and hospitalization in childhood. *Children Today, 3*(4), 12-17.

Bergen, D., Gaynard, L., & Hausslein, E. (1987). Designing special play environments. In Bergen (ed.). *Play as a medium for learning and development*. Portsmouth, N.H.: Heinemann.

Betz, C., & Poster, E. (1984). Incorporating play in the care of the hospitalized child. *Issues in Comprehensive Pediatric Nursing, 7*, 343-355.

Bolig, R. (1984). Play in hospital settings. In T. Yawdey and A. Pellegrini (Eds.). *Play: Developmental and applied*. Hillsdale, NJ: Earlbaum.

Bolig, R. (1990). Play in heath care settings: A challenge for the 1990's. *Children's Health Care, 19*(4), 229-233.

Brazelton, T.B. (1976). Emotional needs of children in health care settings. *Clinical Proceedings of the Children's Hospital National Medical Center, 32*, 137-166.

Chan, J. (1980). Preparation for procedures and surgery through play. *Pediatrician, 9*, 210-219.

D'Antonio, I. (1984). Therapeutic use of play in hospitals. *Nursing Clinic of North America, 19*(2), 351-359.

Elkins, P.D., & Roberts, M.C. (1983). *Psychological preparation for pediatric hospitalizations. Clinical Psychology Review, 3*, 275-295.

Goldberger, J. (1984). The use of toys with hospitalized children. *Children's Environments Quarterly, 2*(3), 57-62.

Hall, D. & Cleary, J. (1988). The development of play for children in hospitals: British and European perspectives. *Children's Health Care, 16*(3), 223-230.

King, J., & Ziegler, S. (1981). The effects of hospitalization on children's behavior: A review of the literature. *Children's Health Care, 10*, 20-28.

Kleinberg, S. (1987). Child life in the 1990's: Changing roles, changing times. *Children's Health Care, 15*, 240-241.

McCue, K. (1988). Medical play: An expanded perspective. *Children's Health Care, 16*(3), 157-161.

Newman, L., & Lind, J. (1980). The child in the hospital: Early stimulation and therapy through play. *Pediatrician, 9*, 147-150.

Oremland, E.K., (1988). Mastering developmental and critical experiences through play and other expressive behaviors in childhood. *Children's Health Care, 16*(3), 150-156.

Petrillo, M., & Sanger, S. (1980). *Emotional care of hospitalized children*. Philadelphia: Lippincott.

Rodin, J. (1983). *Will this hurt? Preparing children for hospital and medical procedures*. London: Royal College of Nursing.

Thompson, R. & Stanford, G. (1981). *Child life in hospitals*. Charles C. Thomas, Springfield, IL.

Vessey, J.A., & Mahon, M.M. (1990). Therapeutic play and hospitalized child. *Journal of Pediatric Nursing of Pediatric Nursing, 5*(5), 328-333.

PEGGY JESSEE, PH.D., is an assistant professor of

human development and families studies at The University of Alabama. She teachers undergraduate and graduate courses in child life. Jane Love is a child life specialist at University Hospitals in Birmingham, Alabama. She is a graduate of the Child Life Program at The University of Alabama. Desiree Derouin is a doctoral student at the University of Illinois, Urbana, Ill. She received her master's degree in child life from the University of Alabama and her undergraduate degree from Purdue University.

Chapter 7
Play in the Health Care Setting:
Prescription for Fun

Jacqueline B. Vogel

The importance of play in the life of the child is well known and extensively documented. Play has a special and unique value, however, for the hospitalized child. The importance of play to the child in the health care setting can best be understood when viewed in the context of how illness and encounters with the health care system affect the young child.

Entry into the world of "high-tech" medicine is often an abrupt and sometimes a traumatic interruption in the normal life of the child. In place of the familiar world of home, family, and friends is a new world filled with strange sights, sounds and smells, a world peopled by strangers who sometimes inflict pain that the child does not comprehend, except perhaps as punishment for some imagined transgression.

The size and scope of the modern medical center can be overwhelming even before treatment of the child begins. Many children first enter a hospital *via* an emergency room, a route that may preclude preparation for the visit and one that may also result in parents so distressed that they have difficulty adequately comforting their child.

Even a planned clinic visit or an admission for elective surgery can arouse considerable anxiety in both child and parent. Paperwork and waiting add to anticipatory anxiety. Once admitted, the child may find that a hospital room is considerably different from his own room at home. The beds are shiny stainless steel and there are side rails on the big beds as well as on the cribs!

Going from place to place in the hospital may involve the new experience of riding in a wheelchair or on a stretcher — even if you are able to walk! The child may also discover that many strange people come and go from his room. Some may knock, introduce themselves, and explain why they are there. Some may not!

The young child in the health care setting is clearly at risk for some emotional distress. Provision for age-appropriate play, however, can do much to relieve the stress and anxiety that otherwise frequently accompanies health care. Play in the health care setting allows the child to continue with as many aspects of normal healthy growth as his medical condition permits. Play supports emerging developmental skills. The active two-year-old who typically learns by physically exploring the environment is at great risk developmentally if illness or immobility keep her bound to the crib. A toddler attached to a ventilator or an intravenous pump is powerless to experience the joy of exploration unless adults take special care to bring such experiences to her bedside. The preschooler ready to discover the world of color, shape, and texture cannot afford to put such experiences "on hold" during illness or hospitalization. The school-aged child and even the adolescent need the stimulation and comfort that can be found in peer relationships whether at home or in the hospital.

Health care settings are notorious for creating feelings of dependency in children as well as in adults. The patient role involves letting others provide care, offer advice, and, in many cases, make decisions. Because illness or trauma may enforce dependency at a time when the child is striving for autonomy, play activities should encourage feelings of control and competence. When children make choices in play, they exchange the passive, dependent patient role for the active assertiveness of the healthy child. Because children in health care settings are not able to decide about the course of their treatment, or even their daily routines, choices in play take on special meaning and value.

The hospital often also acts to depersonalize the patient. Children may find themselves referred to by the name of their disease or by their room number rather than by their own name. It is not uncommon to hear staff refer to a patient as "the brain tumor in 661." Children in hospital playrooms often take great pains to label their artwork with their own names — a precious symbol of self! Children also often label their doors and decorate them with paint.

Illness or hospitalization can arouse many feelings in children just as it does for adults. Children may feel anxiety, anger, sadness, fear, or guilt in reaction to medical care. Pain, separation from home and familiar surroundings, intrusive procedures and/or the use of restraints are all likely to be interpreted by young children as punishment meted out by powerful adults. The young child is not cognitively able to comprehend that a treatment that hurts is actually meant to help. Being held down for a procedure or an injection can provoke a great deal of anger in children. Play allows children to safely express their feelings either in actions or words. The child in the playroom can punch or pound play dough or even loudly assert "I hate doctors and shots" without fear of losing the acceptance of the staff there. Play enables the child to recreate, to some extent, the familiar world of home, family, and friends. Familiar activities reassure and comfort children.

Loss of body function due to illness or trauma is enormously stressful for children. Much of the health care experience focuses on what is wrong with the child. Play can reassure the ill or injured child that part of him "still works." Even when the child is confined to bed, attached to a ventilator, or in traction, play can come to the bedside adapted to the child's unique needs. If hands are restrained to prevent unintentional extubation, a baby or toddler can explore toys or active a musical toy by using feet instead. Bubbles can be popped with toes as well as fingers. Colorful pictures or a properly-positioned mirror can enrich the visual environment. For the child in an intensive care unit following surgery, play materials at the bedside communicate the message "we expect you to get better" even before the child is actually able to actively play. For many a weary parent, the child's first

attempts to play after illness or surgery signals that recuperation is beginning.

Play for children in the health care setting can be an effective means of achieving mastery over new and potentially frightening experiences. Children use play to help them understand and assimilate new information. Medical play with dolls, puppets, or the use of specially-designed story-telling can help the child cope with medical events and procedures. Play can be used to discuss body changes, explain about scars or incisions, or to demonstrate equipment used in the care of the child. A child scheduled for respiratory treatments involving a mask over the mouth and nose will benefit from seeing, touching, and being able to manipulate the mask either on himself or on a doll prior to treatment. Sometimes the use of a doll or puppet may be the only way a child can tolerate such information since it may be too overwhelming in reference to the child's own body. Post-procedural play can help "detoxify" a frightening experience for a young child, just as talking about the experience may serve the same purpose for an adolescent or adult.

Post-procedural play can give staff some insight into what the child has understood about procedures that have been done. By listening to children and observing their play, misconceptions the children have about medical events can be recognized and addressed.

Observations of children at play in the health care setting can also assist the staff with diagnosis. The silent, noncommunicative child seen in the treatment room may appear quite different during a nonthreatening play session. An assessment of developmental level may be easier to obtain and more accurate as well if observation is incorporated into the play experience.

Play serves the child in many ways in the hospital or at home. Parents should be part of the team when planning for a child's play needs in the health care setting. Interacting through play is a normal, natural role for parents and is often a welcome relief for a parent immersed in the tasks of daily physical caregiving for a child with special needs. The joyful and creative aspects of play offer special rewards for these parents.

Many parents have questions or concerns

about siblings. The brothers and sisters of hospitalized children often experience symptoms of stress. Siblings may need to be prepared for the child's homecoming — possibly with altered appearance or accompanied by unfamiliar equipment. Dramatic play with dolls or puppets, story-telling, and other play techniques can be planned to help siblings adjust to new situations.

Transition from hospital to home or from one hospital to another can also necessitate preparation of parents and patient. If the child is old enough, stories, dramatic play, and rehearsal of upcoming events can ease the transition. For example, a camera can be used to create a scrapbook to prepare the patient or siblings for events that might otherwise threaten to overwhelm.

Careful planning can help to eliminate barriers to age-appropriate play in the health care setting. While the large size of the medical center may be initially frightening to both child and parent, visible signs that indicate that children are welcome can go a long way toward easing the child's entry into the clinic or hospital. Long, institutional corridors are less intimidating if colorful children's artwork is prominently displayed on the walls. The presence of adequately equipped, professionally-staffed play spaces, both indoors and out, are further evidence of an institution's support of the critical role of play. If a child entering the health care setting can see play materials and spaces designed for play, the clear message to both child and parents is that "the child's need to play is taken seriously here." The absence of such provisions sends a powerful message as well and it will be felt by child and parent.

Additional Readings about Play in the Health Care Setting

Azarnoff, P. (1975). *A pediatric play program.* Springfield, Ill.: C. C. Thomas.

Caplan, F. & Caplan, T. (1974). *The power of play.* New York: Doubleday.

Clatworth, S. (1981). Therapeutic play: Effects on hospitalized children. *Children's Health Care, 9*(4), 108-113.

Gellert, E. (Ed.). (1978). *Psychosocial aspects of pediatric care.* New York: Grune & Stratton.

Goodall, J. (1976). Opening windows into a child's mind. *Developmental Medicine and Child Neurology, 18,* 173-181.

Gnus, M. (1973). A therapeutic play session in a health center. *Maternal-Child Nursing Journal, 2-3,* 197-201.

Harvey, S. (1975). Play for children in hospitals. *International Journal of Early Childhood, 7,* 185-187.

Harvey, S. & Hales-Tooke, A. (Eds.). (1972). *Play in hospital.* London: Faber and Faber.

Hofmann, A., Becker, R., & Gabriel, H. (1976). *The hospitalized adolescent: A guide to managing the ill and injured youth.* New York: The Free Press.

Pearson, J. E., Cataldo, M., Tureman, A., Bessman, C., & Rogers, M. C. (1980). Pediatric intensive care unit patients; Effects of play intervention on behavior. *Critical Care Medicine, 8,* 64-67.

Petrillo, M. & Sanger, S. (1980). *Emotional care of hospitalized children.* Philadelphia, Penn.: J. B. Lippincott.

Plank, E. N. (1971). *Working with children in hospitals.* Chicago: Year Book Medical Publishers.

Thompson, R. & Stanford, G. (1981). *Child life in hospitals.* Springfield, Ill.: C. C. Thomas.

JACQUELINE B. VOGEL, M.S., C.C.L.S., has been director of the Child Life Program at Texas Children's Hospital since its inception in 1975.

Chapter 8
Integrated Play Experiences for Children with Developmental Disabilities and Respite for Families

ANGELINA MERENDA O'BAR
TERRY JOHNSEN

The past two decades have seen major changes in services to children with disabilities. Historically, children with severe developmental disabilities were placed in institutions with limited access by their families. The expectations for children with disabilities in terms of learning, playing, community involvement, family participation, and individual development were minimal.

Findings from longitudinal stuides following the Community Mental Health Act of 1963 indicated that children and their families showed improved functioning in a community-based setting outside the confinement of an institution. Policy was established on the federal level that reflected these findings (DiNitto and Dye, 1991). Legislation moved responsibility for the care of children from institutions to their families and local communities.

This is a philosophical as well as legal change that recognizes that the family is the constant factor in the lives of children. Making the family the primary caregiver, in the least restrictive environment, gives the child a place in the community and the chance to become as independent and productive as possible. Besides being the more humane of the two approaches, it is the more efficient and cost-effective.

The Developmental Disabilities Assistance and Bill of Rights Act of 1990, Public Law 101-496, defines developmental disability as a severe, chronic disability of a person five years of age or older which:

1. Is attributable to a mental or physical impairment or a combination of mental and physical impairments
2. Is manifested before the person attains age twenty-two
3. Is likely to continue indefinitely
4. Results in substantial functional limitations in three or more of the following areas of major life activity: self-care; receptive and expressive language; learning; mobility; self-direction; capacity for independent living; and economic self-sufficiency
5. Reflects the person's need for a combination and sequence of special interdisciplinary or generic care, treatment, or other services which are of lifelong or of extended duration and are individually planned and coordinated.

Infants and young children, meaning individuals from birth through five years, who have substantial developmental delay or specific congenital or acquired conditions, are likely to have developmental disabilities if services are not provided. The trend today is to promote normal patterns of living by assisting the developmentally disabled through community-based family support services. Pre-school early intervention, special education within schools, and community agencies all can help young citizens and their families with special needs. Although legislation provides for multiple services for families of children with developmental disabilities, families have a great need for emotional support to help develop a sense of control of their lives. The lack of specific skills to cope with the unique needs of a developmentally disabled child and a lack of understanding about how to obtain help from agencies are among the factors that cause compounding problems. Divorce, financial crisis, family violence, child abuse and neglect, alcohol and drug abuse, and other stress-related problems are common outcomes that many families must live with daily.

The Chickasha Project

A community-based program for families of young children with developmental disabilities, The Chickasha Project (TCP) was initiated in Oklahoma in 1990. The mandate of TCP was to develop a demonstration model which rural communities could replicate, to publish and disseminate a handbook based on the model, and to offer technical assistance to other communities. TCP was designed to:

1. Promote community awareness of the importance of early intervention in identifying children with developmental disabilities
2. Assist families in the identification of their specific needs in order to acquire skills needed to work with children more effectively
3. Promote mental wellness for familiy members through a network of service agencies, support groups and respite care
4. Recruit and train individuals to assist with the care of children during respite group care sessions, at schools and in their homes
5. Help families make health adjustments to home-based care for children with severe developmental disabilities
6. Work within the existing network of services to eliminate perceived barriers and facilitate family use of community resources.

TCP sponsors guest speakers, workshops, and seminars focusing on family counseling, behavior and guidance, child development, the importance of early intervention, and advocacy. Community seminars, radio, newspapers, billboards and other promotional events are used to increase community awareness of the importance of early identification of developmental disabilities in young children and to recruit families and volunteers.

To help meet the needs of families, TCP organized and continues to sponsor a family support group, a Dads' Support Group, and "I'm Special Too!", a support group designed to meet the needs of siblings of children with developmental disabilities. Support groups meet monthly with respite care and activities provided for children during the meetings.

One of the project's most successful activities is Time Out for Parents. This activity provides parents with an opportunity for respite. These regular Saturday afternoon programs provide a reprieve for parents from the emotional and physical demands of raising a child with special needs. They give parents time for their own personal and social needs. There is no charge for Time Out for Parents. Parents are encouraged to leave all of their children if they want the time just for themselves, or just the child with the disability if they wish to spend special time with their other children.

Time Out for Parents offers children planned, integrated, recreational activities under the guidance of professionals and specially-trained volunteers. The project draws volunteers from the community, students attending Chickasha public schools, students of allied health from a local vocational school, and students from nearby colleges. Volunteers are used in all activities and are vital to the success of the project.

While some children with severe disabilities need special equipment, most can play with the same toys, games, and materials available for other children. The selection of toys, games, or materials depends on the specific needs of the individual children participating in respite program activities.

These suggestions can help others plan respite programs:

1. The way you introduce an activity and materials is important. Most children respond better if they see someone else use the materials first.
2. Choose materials that can be used by children at different developmental levels. Any group of children will have varying ability levels for a particular activity. When working with children with disabilities, you need to expand the range of abilities you usually think about.
3. Limit the items available for use; too many toys or materials can be very distracting.
4. You may need to adapt the toys and materials so a child with special needs can use them more easily.
   - Keep materials from slipping off the table or other surface. Tape, Velcro®, and suction cup holders are some ways to keep

things from slipping.
- Make handles bigger or add handles to things without them. (Use foam bike handle grips; make a pad with cotton and cover with tape; put cork stoppers or dowels on puzzle pieces.)
- Make eating more independent by bending spoon handles and using flexible straws and non-tipping or spouted cups with lids. Use highly contrasting colors or heavy black outlines for children with visual impairments.
- Put a bell inside a foam ball to help a child with limited vision play ball with others.
- Provide stiffer string or cover ends of string with masking tape for beading.
- Cover paper materials (books, cards) with clear adhesive paper to make them easier to handle and more durable.
- Add textured cues (sandpaper, fake fur, vinyl) to help blind children locate items.
- Use picture cues to show how materials are used or to help children tell you what they want.
- Use ramps, stairs, and railings to help children reach sinks, toilets, and shelves.

The Chickasha Project included publication of a manual to enable communities to adapt TCP for their own use. The manual describes the steps in the process and includes sample forms and resource materials. It is for families, professionals, volunteers, and other concerned citizens wanting to start a support group in their communities.

State and Federal Support

Various state and federal programs can provide services and equipment to support families of children with disabilities in their homes and communities. In Oklahoma, the Disabled Children's Program in the Department of Human Services assists families in providing services and equipment for children who qualify for and receive Supplemental Security Income (SSI). (SSI is a federal payment to children with disabilities.) This program receives federal matching funds through the Maternal and Child Health Block Grant. It provides services to children from birth through 16 years through the 79 county offices of the DHS. Each child has a caseworker who works with the family to assess needs and establish a service plan.

A part of the ongoing service plan for each child is to provide, without cost to the family, services and equipment that are not compensable through other programs such as Medicaid. The SSI-Disabled Children's Program provides adaptive equipment, environmental aids, diapers, formula, and developmental aids and toys for home use. The program recognizes the importance of developing skills and competency through play with toys and developmental aids. The program provides toys to enhance learning through creative play.

The program allocates approximately one third of its budget for the purchase of educational equipment and toys. The program serves more than 4,500 children in Oklahoma.

References

Bailey, D. B. & Simeonsson, R. J. (1988). Family assessment in early intervention. Columbus, Ohio: Merrill.

Bresnick, D. A. (1983). Managing the human services in hard times. New York: Human Services Press.

DiNitto, D. M. & Dye, T. R. (1985). Social welfare: Politics and public policy. New York: Prentice-Hall.

ANGELINA MERENDA O'BAR, M.A., is associate director of the Center for Child and Family Development at the University of Oklahoma. TERRY JOHNSEN, M.S.W., is coordinator of the Disabled Children's Program of the Oklahoma Department of Human Services.

Part III
Children's Play: Role Examinations

The existence and value of socio-dramatic play are well documented in the literature. Without adequate opportunities for socio-dramatic play, children suffer cognitively, emotionally, socially, and physically. Therefore, the examination of the importance of role-playing in the lives of children is critical. The papers in this section look at the socio-dramatic play of at-risk toddlers, discuss the use of props to encourage socio-dramatic play, and propose some new dimensions of socio-dramatic play for study and observation.

All children play. We learn exactly what that means by focusing on the specific types of play in different populations. **Bergen's** study is one of the few studies that has focused on symbolic and social play of at-risk toddlers. The observational study of seven children found that emerging social play (onlooking and parallel) with adults appeared to be the predominant kind of play. Implications include the importance of social peer models of at-risk toddlers, inclusion of play observation for assessment, and the importance of planning play-based learning opportunities in early intervention.

Socio-dramatic is the most highly developed form of play. But what can educators do to encourage and ensure children reach this highest level? **Hatcher, Nicosia,** and **Pape** provide an excellent overview of the role socio-dramatic play in development and ways to facilitate socio-dramatic play through theme and prop boxes.

"What's going on here?", the question asked by many teachers, was the general question asked formally by the researcher. In continuing to study socio-dramatic play, **Steffey** proposes four lesser known, but compelling dimensions of socio-dramatic play: child-selected activity, tendency to play in pairs, pretense within pretense, and insider perspective. Each of these provide a new way to study the multi-faceted, sophisticated, and fascinating socio-dramatic play of young children.

Chapter 9
Symbolic and Social Play of At-risk Young Children in an Inclusive Environment

DORIS BERGEN

Although studies of the play of typically developing toddlers show that the preponderant type observed is sensorimotor practice (Bergen, 1988), symbolic play usually appears between the ages of 12 to 15 months and evidence of some type of pretend is an expected developmental milestone by 20 months of age (Bretherton et al., 1984; Nelson & Seidman, 1984; Nicholich, 1977). Studies of young children with disabilities or developmental delay indicate that most of these children begin to exhibit symbolic play when they reach the mental age of approximately 20 months. The presence of toddler-level language ability (i.e., two word utterances; understanding of "no," and understanding that objects can have names) has also been found to be related to symbolic play ability (Casby & Ruder, 1983).

Social interaction with adults appears to facilitate early development of symbolic play. For example, studies of mother and child play indicate that toddlers learn to play roles by engaging in pretend play with their mothers and that by age three can perform the roles of mother and baby (Miller & Garvey, 1984). By the age of three, typically developing toddlers can engage not only in social pretend play with an adult but can interact symbolically in pretend with siblings and peers (Dunn and Kendrick, 1981; Howes, 1988).

Although there have been some studies of the early symbolic and social play of at-risk preschoolers (e.g., Beckman & Kohl, 1984; Fitzgerald, 1985; Mindes, 1982; Terrell & Schwartz, 1988), few studies have focused on the toddler-age range. The research on three-to five-year-old children with identified disabilities show that their social play with peers is generally less extensive than that of typically-developing chil-

dren. However, the presence of peers who are not delayed enhances the opportunities for social interaction of the at-risk children. The types of toys that are available also appear to have an effect on the likelihood of social interactions.

The body of literature on play development (reviewed by Bergen, 1988; Rubin, Fein, & Vandenberg, 1983) points clearly to the importance of play development for other developmental domains (e.g., cognitive, language, social, emotional and physical). Information on the frequency and characteristics of symbolic and social play of young children at risk for developmental delay could make those domain relationships clearer. It could also provide assistance to early interventionists as they use play-based assessment, design and foster play-based curriculum opportunities, and identify adult play-based instructional techniques that facilitate the development of important precursors to academic learning.

The study reported here is one phase of an ongoing research project. It describes the symbolic and social play and other social interactions of a group of young children who were participants in an inclusive early childhood program on the Miami University campus in the spring of 1992. The study involves collection of both naturalistic observation data and laboratory-elicited play data from children at this site and at two non-inclusive early intervention sites (12 classrooms), as well as three toddler child care programs primarily serving typically developing children (five classrooms).

The following questions were of interest:

1. What proportion of the activity events that occur in the setting will show evidence of symbolic and/or social play?
2. What types of symbolic and social play will occur?

3. Will the symbolic play of young children who have been identified as at risk for developmental delay be similar in quantity and duration to that of the typically developing children of comparable chronological age?
4. Will the social interactive play and the nonplay social interactions of these children be similar in quantity and duration?
5. Will social interaction with adults be more frequent than social interaction with peers?
6. Will older and younger children's play patterns differ?

Methodology

The subject are seven children of 24 to 41 months who participated in the inclusive early intervention program on the Miami University (Ohio) campus. Two have no identification as at-risk (the "typical" children) and six children were referred to the program after diagnosis of potential for developmental delay. Two children are at-risk because of environmental conditions (abuse or neglect); one has both a language delay and a physical disability (upper limbs); one is biologically at-risk (birth trauma, medically fragile), and one is at-risk because of

a severe language delay (foreign-born).

The seven children in the study were videotaped during the program day in a randomly assigned order, with each child being observed for ten minutes on each occasion until a total of 40-50 minutes per child were collected. (Variations occurred because of absences.) The children were familiar with the video camera because it is used regularly at the center for analyses of university student practicum experiences.

Emerging social play (onlooking and parallel) appeared to be the predominant kind of play for all but the oldest typical child. That child engaged in social play 30% of the time and this play involved peers in more than half of the social play incidents. Three of the at-risk children spent over 80% of their social play engaged with adults rather than peers; two at-risk children and the younger typical child engaged with adults about 70% of the time. The oldest at-risk child had a slightly higher proportion (58%) of social play interactions with adults than with peers and showed about an equal distribution of interactions with typical and at-risk children.

Two children, the oldest at-risk child and the oldest typical child (the former one month

Social Play	Cognitive Play		
	Practice	Symbolic	Games
Onlooking	17% (SD=7)	.7% (SD-1.2)	3.4% (SD=3.9)
Solitary	13.4% (SD=4)	4.7% (SD=3.5)	0% (SD=0)
Parallel	14.9% (SD=5.4)	3% (SD=2.2)	2.1% (SD=2.9)
Associative	9.7% (SD=3.8)	6.4% (SD=4.7)	2.7% (Sd=2.9)
Cooperative	0% (SD=0)	0% (SD=0)	0% (SD=0)

Table 1: Average proportion of play types in total number of events.
*Of all events, 25% did not include play.

older than the latter), accounted for approximately half (48%) of the total symbolic play recorded. However, their symbolic play had a different social quality. The highest proportion of the at-risk child's symbolic play was solitary (46%) while the typical child's symbolic play was primarily associative (70%).

The children used realistic objects (cooking utensils, dress-up clothes, suitcase, purses) more than 10 times as often in the symbolic play, although ambiguous (clay), counterconventional (pan as baseball bat), and imaginary objects were all used in object transformations at least five times. They took few actual roles; however, family roles and occupational roles were seen briefly, with one animal role being enacted. The schemes most often seen were cooking and eating and telephone communication, with caring for dolls and other children, other home activities, and work (fireman, carpenter) schemes also used. Aggressive schemes were used on a number of occasions (primarily "gun" shooting using ambiguous objects.) Another symbolic scheme involved "reading" or "writing" with paper, shaving cream, and books.

Adult roles that encouraged play were similar to those described by Miller and Garvey (1984). In their study, they identified eight ways that mothers of toddler girls assisted their children's symbolic play. The adults in the early intervention setting showed many of these same behaviors at least once. In the classroom they had created a context for symbolic play and provided many props for children to use in symbolic play. They also conveyed acceptance of children's pretend play with objects (by observing, smiling, giving them props); provided some verbal commentary about the children's symbolic play activities; responded positively to children's initial engagement as play partners; and expanded the symbolic quality of the play. However, they gave few explicit instructions regarding how to pretend.

This study provides some information about the symbolic play of children in one inclusive early intervention program. The children showed generally typical types of play, with practice play being predominant and emerging social interactions most frequently recorded within events. Symbolic play was recorded in

slightly fewer than one third of the play events and of all events, play was recorded in three-fourths of these. Only one fourth of the play events were of a truly socially interactive nature.

The older children, at-risk and typical, showed the greatest amount of symbolic play although the social quality of that play differed, with only the oldest typical child showing mainly socially interactive symbolic play. When symbolic play was observed in the at-risk children, its character was relatively similar to that for typically developing children; however, observations showed a delay in onset and/or frequency of symbolic play in most of the younger children.

A smaller proportion of socially interactive peer play was seen in most of the at-risk children. When peer play did occur, however, the proportion of events that showed interaction with typical peers or with at-risk peers was similar for all socially interactive children.

The strategies used by adults to foster symbolic play were also similar to those used by mothers of typical toddlers. The adults did not attempt to foster symbolic play in all of the toddlers, however, but directed their facilitation strategies toward those children who were already exhibiting some spontaneous symbolic play.

Peers as Social Models

Within the limitations imposed by the small number of subjects and limited observation time period, there are a number of implications that can inform early intervention practice and/or suggest further study. First, the results indicating that the typically developing young children showed more involvement in social play suggest that the presence of typically developing peers may provide social models for children who are developmentally at-risk. The typically developing peers were not only more socially interactive generally but were also more socially interactive with peers in their symbolic play. The presence of these children may thus facilitate play development both through their direct interactions with the at-risk children and through the models of social interaction that they provide with their typical peers.

A second implication of this study is that observation of symbolic and social play developmental levels may be an essential part of early intervention assessment procedures. Because the time of typical onset of symbolic and social play and the stages through which the play progresses are well documented, play-based assessment can give early interventionists insights into young children's developmental strengths and delays.

A third implication of this type of study is that early interventionists who are aware of the developmental play levels of children will be able to plan play-based learning opportunities and use effective play-facilitation strategies to foster symbolic and social play development. Sometimes insufficient attention is given in early intervention programs to faclitating play development because teacher-directed functional skill development is of major concern. Specific analysis of the at-risk toddler's play and social development can be useful in planning intervention strategies. For example, intervention strategies and goals may be different for children who show typical, although somewhat delayed, patterns of social and symbolic play, as compared to strategies and goals for children who show very little or very distorted patterns of these types of play. Selection of the appropriate adult facilitation strategy and the most effective method of involving peers in social interactions will depend on a good understanding of these developmental factors.

Finally, the modeling of symbolic play facilitation strategies by teachers could also result in better parental fostering of symbolic play development at home. Because adult facilitation strategies enhance symbolic play development in typically developing toddlers, parents of toddlers who are at-risk need to be assisted in using these effective strategies as well.

Both longitudinal and cross-sectional studies with larger samples must be conducted and a number of inclusive settings must be compared to non-inclusive settings if the value of typical peer social interaction with at-risk toddlers is to be effectively evaluated. Study of how the presence of typically playing toddler peers may enhance not only play development but also other areas of development are also needed.

References

Beckman, P.J. & Kohl, F.L. (1984). The effects of social and isolate toys on the interactions and play of integrated and nonintegrated groups of preschoolers. *Education and Training of the Mentally Retarded, 19,* 169-174.

Bergen, D. (1988). Methods for studying play. In D. Bergen (Ed.) *Play as a medium for learning and development* (pp. 27-44). Portsmouth, NH: Heinemann.

Bretherton, I., O'Connell, B., Shore, C., & Bates, E. (1984). The effect of contextual variation on symbolic play: Development from 20 to 28 months. In I. Bretherton, (Ed.), *Symbolic play: The development of social understanding* (pp. 271-298), New York: Academic Press.

Casby, M.W., & Ruder, K.F. (1983). Symbolic play and early language development in normal and mentally retarded children. *Journal of Speech and Hearing Research, 26*(3), 404-411.

Dunn, J., & Kendrick, C. (1981). Social behavior of young siblings in the family context: Differences between same-sex and different-sex dyads. *Child Development, 52,* 1265-1273.

Fitzgerald, N.B. (1985). Competencies and contexts of friendship development in a reverse mainstreamed preschool. Paper presented at AREA, Chicago, April. (ERIC Document Reproduction No. ED 262 876).

Howes, C. (1988). Peer interaction of young children. *Monographs of the Society for Research in Child Development, 53*(1), 1-88.

Miller, P., & Garvey, C. (1984). Mother-baby role play: Its origins in social support. In I. Bretherton, (Ed.), *Symbolic play: The development of social understanding* (pp. 101-130). New York: Academic Press.

Mindes, G. (1982). Social and cognitive aspects of play in young handicapped children. *Topics in Early Childhood Special Education, 2*(3), 39-52.

Nelson, K., & Seidman, S. (1984). Playing with scripts. In I. Bretherton, (Ed.), *Symbolic play: The development of social understanding* (pp. 45-72). New York: Academic Press.

Nicholich, L.M. (1977). Beyond sensorimotor intelligence: Assessment of symbolic maturity through analysis of pretend play. *Merrill-Palmer Quarterly, 23*(2), 89-99.

O'Connell, B. & Bretherton, I. (1984). Toddler's play alone and with mother: The role of maternal guidance. In I. Bretherton, (Ed.), *Symbolic play: The development of social understanding* (pp. 45-72). New York: Academic Press.

Rubin, K. H., Fein, G. G., & Vandenberg, B. (1983). Play. In E. M. Hetherington (Ed.) & P. H. Mussen (Series Ed.), *Handbook of child psychology: Vol. 4; Socialization, personality, and social development* (pp. 698-774). New York: Wiley.

Terrell, B.Y., & Schwartz, R.G. (1988). Object transformations in the play of language-impaired children. *Journal of Speech and Hearing Disorders, 53,* 459-466.

DORIS BERGEN is professor and chair, Department of Educational Psychology, Miami University, Oxford, Ohio. She has taught a wide range of early childhood, human development, and educational psychology courses, including courses on play development and therapy, development of infants and toddlers, and early intervention assessment and educational planning. Her research interests have included studies of the play, humor, and social development of young children and cultural comparative studies on early childhood educators' views of appropriate teaching practice. She is past president of the National Association of Early Childhood Teacher Educators and a board member of the National Association for the Education of Young Children Professional Development Institute.

Chapter 10
Using Props to Encourage Sociodramatic Play

Barbara Hatcher
R. Tim Nicosia
Dianne Rush Pape

The most highly developed form of symbolic play is sociodramatic play. In dramatic play children assume roles, imitating actions and speech they have observed. When two or more children act together, the play becomes sociodramatic. Children must cooperate and communicate as they enact a story line or plot related to the chosen roles (Garvey, 1977).

Sociodramatic play contains two elements. The first element is the imitative one in which children imitate real-life people and situations that they have observed or experienced. This is the element of reality. However, because of children's inability to imitate exactly what they observe, a second element, that of pretense or make-believe, enters their play. Make-believe aids in imitation and gives children satisfaction by enabling them to enter the world of adults (Smilansky, 1968).

Although the beginnings of sociodramatic play appear by two-and-one-half years of age, children usually do not engage in fully elaborated sociodramatic play until they are four or five years old. What begins as a few simple gestures progresses to become an intricate system of reciprocal roles, ingenious improvisations with materials, and incredibly coherent themes and plots (Fein, 1979). Sociodramatic play comes to a peak around ages four, five, and six and fades away by seven years. Christie and Wardel (1992) explain that sociodramatic play is important because it is a prelude to experiences which children will later have firsthand.

Value of Sociodramatic Play

What can children learn from sociodramatic play? Vygotsky (1976) claims so-

ciodramatic play significantly contributes to children's cognitive and social development. He believes this type of play has an important role in the development of abstract, logical thought. Beaty (1992) suggests that through sociodramatic play young children learn cooperation, prosocial values such as honesty, service, loyalty, and truthfulness, how to gain entrance to a group, how to be a leader, how to deal with a strong leader, how to negotiate, and how to deal with people with whom you disagree. Sociodramatic play promotes concepts such as work, play, order, and time, travel and transportation, illness, doctors, emergencies, roles of family members and workers, problem solving, and how to view things from another's point of view.

Linguistically, sociodramatic play promotes practice in conversing, how to speak as a different character, how to express feelings in words, the uses and meanings of new words, and the use of words as a substitute for actions. Emotionally, sociodramatic play nurtures a positive self-concept, enables children to express strong feelings in acceptable ways, provides opportunities to deal with conflict and control, divergent thinking, novel solutions to problems and flexibility (Beaty, 1992). Smilansky found sociodramatic play improves children's social skills, enhances symbolic capabilities, stimulates language development, broadens concepts, and leads to the acquisition of knowledge (1968). The implications are clear. Thinking, play, and language grow with expanding sociodramatic engagements and with partner play (Singer and Singer, 1977).

Sociodramatic Play Requires Time

Rich sociodramatic play involves role-playing, the use of symbols, interaction, persistence, and verbal communication (Smilansky,

1968). As a result, this type of play requires skills and time to play and initiate. Prior to the start of group dramatic play, children must recruit others to play, negotiate the roles to be enacted, act on the storyline to be dramatized, designate the make-believe identities of objects, and determine the location of play. Group dramatic play can have several false starts as children jockey for positions or other children enter the play. A minimum of 30 minutes is required for many children to progress through preparatory activities and arrive at group dramatic play (Christie and Wardel, 1992). It is noteworthy that Christie's and Wardel's research confirms the importance of sustained periods of time for play, but these investigators also suggest that the lack of appropriate materials and negative teacher attitudes toward play directly impacts the level and quality of young children's play (1992).

Sociodramatic Play Requires Props and Materials

Can props and materials enhance the quality of sociodramatic play? Beaty (1992) and Seefeldt and Barbour (1990) believe props make a difference. "If there are no telephones in the center, there will be little telephoning" (Beaty, 1992, p. 260). Bender (1972) suggests that sociodramatic play can be encouraged through the use of props organized around themes. She believes that props and prop boxes lead to excellent beginning concepts of occupational opportunities. "They are work oriented. They beautifully supplement spontaneous role-playing of any sort. A prop box contains the kinds of things which prevent play from becoming stale or from stopping altogether" (Bender, 1972, p. 44).

McLoyd (1986) encourages the use of both high-realism and low-realism toys and props in play in order to accommodate differing stages of children's development. The range of play materials and toys should include items that are flexible, open-ended or nontheme-specific. Conversely, there is a need to balance role-playing with materials which are theme-specific. Zeece and Graul (1990) further suggest that sociodramatic play props should be changed frequently and related to children's real-life experiences. Use of different props allows children to enact a variety of life experiences and to

determine how these experiences affect them.

Finally, Seefeldt and Barbour (1990) recommend that the dramatic play area reflect the child's community, home, and culture. Materials in the dramatic play area should promote development of both expressive and written language. The area should include more than just housekeeping; props for a play office, gas station, fast-food restaurant, gardening center, and anything that offers children an opportunity to re-enact their experiences is helpful.

Suggested Themes and Props for Sociodramatic Play

The provision of judiciously-selected play props can spark interest, engagement, and elaboration of play and language (McKee, 1986; Maxim, 1981; Essa, 1992). Jan Bandich (1988) for example, suggests a restaurant prop box with menus from local eateries, small trays, dishes, glasses, plastic silverware, tablecloth and napkins, chef's hat, waiter's apron and hat, waiter's vest, coffeepot, pads and pencils. By reenacting everyday experiences such as eating out, going on a picnic, washing the clothes or the car, or going to the post office and grocery, children learn to synthesize scattered experiences and create new ones. These role-playing opportunities give practice in disciplining actions in relation to a context and help children grow from egocentric beings to social beings.

Themes and selected prop box items can facilitate children's sociodramatic play. (See lists.)

Guidelines for Prop Selection

What kind of props are appropriate for sociodramatic play? Select props which:
- Encourage both expressive and written language
- Promote social interaction
- Are relevant to children's experiences and interests
- Are manageable in size for children
- Are safe, nontoxic, durable, and washable
- Are inexpensive (peruse garage sales, thrift shops, state and federal surplus facilities, etc.)
- Are nonsexist, nonracial in nature; props and themes should convey a sense of equality and tolerance
- Are attractive and appealing to children

Restaurant

Cookbooks
Chef's hat
Apron
Dish towel
Dish cloth
Hot pads
Rolling pin
Cookie cutters
Doughnut cutter
Cookie sheet
Muffin tin
Gingerbread man pan
Heart-shaped pan
Cake pan
Bread pan
Pitcher
Mixing bowl
Measuring cup
Measuring spoons
Tablecloth
Timer
Funnel
Scoop
Spatula
Pastry brush
Whisk
Large mixing spoon
Cake knife
Recipe file box
Recipe cards
Pencils
Sifter
Egg carton
Cupcake liners
Play dough
Plates
Saucers
Glasses
Cups
Salt shaker
Pepper shaker
Ladle
Cake server
Egg beater
Pot

Laundromat

Toy washer
Toy dryer
Laundry basket
Clothes
Bleach container
Detergent box
Measuring cup
Children's clothes hangers
Clothespins
Open/Closed sign
Hours of operation sign
Toy money

Farm

Toy farm animals
Apron
Work gloves
Shovel
Hoe
Bucket
Wagon
Seeds
Toy barn
Toy tractor
Toy trailer
Visored hats
Toy computer
Toy cellular telephone

Camp

Tent
Rope
Blanket or sleeping bag
Fishing poles
Toy fish
Toy axe
Compass
Flashlights
Backpack
Walkie-talkie
Telescope
Canteen
Stew pot

Mess kit
Wood for campfire
Field guide to birds
Field guide to insects
Ice chest
Toy food

Airplane Travel

Camera
Travel brochures
Toy money
Captain's jacket
Steward's apron
Serving items for meals
Suitcase
Paper
Pencils
Pens
Stamps
Pilot's hat
Magazines
Maps
Seatbelt
Airplane ticket

Veterinarian Clinic

Toy animals
Hypodermics
Scratch paper
Folders
Pencils
Clipboard
White shirts
Bandages
Brush
Towel
Plastic tub
Washcloth

Fire Station

Firefighter's helmet
Firefighter's coat
Firefighter's pants
Firefighter's boots

Props for various types of sociodramatic play.

Rubber hose
City map
Telephones
Goggles

Baseball Park

Baseball shirts
Baseball pants
Baseball bat
Baseballs (or softballs)
Gloves
Baseball hats
Candy boxes
Hotdog containers
Napkins
Toy money
Sunglasses
Sunscreen
Cups
Mustard container
Ketchup container
Relish container

Hat Play

Straw beach hat
Necklace
Ladies' dress hat
Stetson hat
Straw hat
Army officer's hat
Motorcycle helmet
Suitcase
Safari hat
Visored cap
Baseball cap
Scarf
Goggles
Ski cap
Safety helmet

Office

Stickers
Stamps
Pencils

Colored markers
Stamp pad
Rubber stamps
Eraser
Diary
Typing paper
Stationery
Invitations
Postcards
Thank-you notes
Notepads
Birthday cards
Pencil case
Pencil sharpener
Notecards

Nursery

Doll
Doll blanket
Changing pad
Baby clothes
Bib
Bonnet
Bottle
Serving dish
Baby spoon
Pacifier
Bath sponge
Baby lotion
Powder
Diapers
Fresh wipes
Teething ring

Boat

Toy or real boat
Fishing poles
Worms
Flag
Oars
First-aid kit
Life jacket
Towel
Water
Fishing net

Toy fish
Bucket
Shovel
Sand
Sunglasses
Sunscreen
Beach toys

Garden

Seeds
Water jug
Harvesting basket
Gloves
Watering can
Shovel
Rake
Hoe
Toy lawn mower
Sprinkler
Garden hose
Toy or real wheelbarrow
Vegetables
Sunscreen
Plant food
Hats

Grocery Store

Food containers
Shopping basket
Apron
Newspaper advertisements
Coupons
Checkbook
Checks
Toy money
Wallet
Pads of paper
Pencils
Pens
Toy or real cash register
Price tags
Nametags
Sale signs
Brown paper bags
Produce

• Are useful for both indoor and outdoor sociodramatic play

Care of Props and Prop Boxes

Storage, care and maintenance of props and prop boxes is essential. Consider the following ideas when designing prop boxes:
• Label the front of the box and include a picture of the characters associated with the theme. This will help children in the selection process. For example, a restaurant prop box might include a picture of a chef and the name and logo of a restaurant.
• Make boxes easily accessible to children if they are to be used for an extended period.
• Post an itemized list of the props in each box. This will aid in returning misplaced items.
• Store all items related to a theme in a single box, if possible. If items are too large for the container, store in a suitable place.
• Select a sturdy container for props. Decorate with adhesive paper or suitable materials to appeal to children and prolong wear.
• Check boxes periodically to ensure that clothing, wigs, and other items are clean and free from possible contaminants.

Developing a Prop Box Lending Program

If you are interested in establishing a lending program for prop boxes, consider the following:
• Who will be responsible for the boxes? Classroom teacher, school or public library, volunteer parent group, civic club, city parks and recreation department, housing authority committee, or other? Who will store the boxes?
• Who will clean, maintain, and replace props? Develop policies and procedures for lost and damaged items.
• Will there be a charge or refundable deposit for use of boxes? How much?
• Determine a check-out system. This may include check-out cards or forms. What information will you need in order to lend boxes?
• Establish reasonable periods for use of boxes — three days, one week, etc. This may depend on the ages and interests of the children served, check-out and return convenience for parents and caregivers, and other factors.
• Create duplicate or similar prop boxes for

popular and seasonal themes.
• Provide a brief information sheet on how to use and care for each prop box. Keep multiple copies of each sheet available.
• Consider demonstrating how to use boxes for inexperienced but interested users.
• Start small. Develop a reasonable number of thematic boxes well rather than too many without adequate props.

Evaluating Sociodramatic Play with Prop Boxes

Sociodramatic play provides rich opportunities for children's cognitive, affective, and psychomotor development. When evaluating sociodramatic play, educators and parents may look for evidence of:
• Growth in both expressive and receptive language
• Use of new vocabulary as a result of play with props. Are children learning the proper names for items they use in play? Does the play promote print-related actions such as signs, labels, etc.? Does the play reveal pre-reading skills and actions?
• Appropriate use of materials. Do children use props in acceptable ways? Can they identify new and appropriate uses for the items?
• More social play. Are children becoming more cooperative and flexible? Are they more skilled in social interactions such as negotiating, offering alternatives, and resolving disputes and suggesting compromise?
• Planning, organizing, solving problems, and persistence.
• Ease with which children lead, follow, and facilitate roles in play.
• Enhanced self-confidence to try new experiences as a result of the play.
• Preferences in play. Do children prefer highly active, highly imaginative themes or more familiar domestic play themes? Is there a difference in play preferences of girls and boys? Is the same theme enacted repeatedly with greater elaboration and insight? What common play themes occur daily? Weekly? Monthly? Does the play generate questions? What is the nature of the children's questions?

In conclusion, there will always be spontaneous sociodramatic play on the part of children, but wise adults also set the stage for play by providing props and initiating activities. This "pretending" becomes a way for children to investigate their world. Beaty (992) believes that through pretending to be others, children find out what it is like to be themselves. Through pretending to be other places, they find out what it is like to be where they are. A real paradox, but true!

References

Bandich, J. (1988). *Get ready for dramatic play.* Cypress, Calif.: Creative Teaching Press, Inc.

Beaty, J. J. (1992). *Preschool appropriate practices.* New York: Harcourt Brace Jovanovich College Publishers.

Bender, J. (1972). Have you even thought of a prop box? In K. R. Baker (Ed.), *Ideas that work with children* Washington, D.C.: National Association for the Education of Young Children.

Christie, J. F. & Wardel, F. (1992). How much time is needed for play? *Young Children, 47*(3), 28-32.

Essa, E. (1992). *Introduction to early childhood education.* Albany, N.Y.: Delmar.

Fein, G. G. (1979). Play and acquisition of symbols. In L. Katz (Ed.), *Current topics in early childhood* , Vol 2. Norwood, N.J.: Ablex.

Garvey, C. (1977). *Play.* Cambridge, Mass.: Harvard University Press.

Maxim, G. W. (1981). *The sourcebook: Activities to enrich programs for infants and young children.* Belmon, Calif.: Wadsworth Publishing Co.

McKee, J. L. (Ed.) (1986). *Play: Working partner of growth.* Washington, D.C.: Association for Childhood Education International.

McLoyd, V. (1986). Scaffolds or shackles? The role of toys in preschool children's pretend play. In G. Fein and M. Rivkin, Eds, *The young child and play: Review of the research,* Vol. 4. Washington, D.C.: National Association for the Education of Young Children.

Seefeldt, C. & Barbour, N. (1990). *Early childhood education: An introduction.* 2nd edition. New York: Wiley.

Vygotsky, L. S. (1976). Play and its role in the mental development of the child. In J. S. Bruner, A. Jolly, & K. Sylva (Eds.), *Play: Its role in development and evolution.* New York: Basic Books.

Zeece, P. S. & Graul, S. K. (1990). Learning to play: Playing to learn. *Day Care and Early Education, 18*(1), 11-15.

BARBARA HATCHER, ED.D., is a professor of early childhood and elementary education at Southwest Texas State University. R. TIMOTHY NICOSIA, ED.D., is director of elementary and early childhood programs at Southwest Texas State University. DIANNE RUSH PAPE, M.A., is a lecturer and teacher at the Early Childhood Laboratory School at Southwest Texas State University.

Chapter 11
Some Well-known and Not So Well-known Elements
of Sociodramatic Play

M. Stephanie Steffey

Upon entering the housekeeping center after play had already begun, Megan asked the other children, "What's going on here?" This is a question many busy kindergarten teachers may also ask. "What's going on here?" may have a different meaning when asked by parents, school administrators and first-grade teachers. Is the children's time well-spent at sociodramatic play or would it be better spent at more teacher-directed endeavors?

Kindergarten teachers traditionally have supported "housekeeping" play as a form of sociodramatic play. Sociodramatic play occurs when two or more children share in the pretense of acting out roles other than their own. In housekeeping play, the roles typically include those of family members and occasionally the family pet. Domestic life is most often the theme of the play because this is the domain with which young children are most familiar. In the literature, fully-developed sociodramatic play is defined as being composed of six particular elements (Smilansky, 1968; Smilansky & Shefayta, 1990).

1. Imitative role play
2. Make-believe with objects
3. Make-believe with actions and situations
4. Persistence in role
5. Social interaction
6. Verbal communication

These six elements lead to the development of social, cognitive, and social-cognitive skills and concepts associated with future academic and school success (Bateson, 1972; Parten, 1932; Piaget, 1954, 1962; Smilansky, 1968; Smilansky & Shefatya, 1990; Vygotsky, 1962).

It was in response to the question, "What's going on here?", that the formal research reported in this paper was initially undertaken. More specifically, questions addressed were:

1. What are the children doing while in the housekeeping play area?
2. Do their activities support cognitive development?
3. Are the elements of sociodramatic play, as defined by Smilansky (1968) and Smilansky and Shefatya (1990) present in the kindergarten housekeeping play?

The purpose of this paper is twofold: in Part I, to share the results of the formal study addressing the presence of the six elements as outlined above, and in Part II, to present some less familiar elements of play which emerged during the formal study and from less formal pre- and post-study observations.

Part I

Methodology

The setting was a kindergarten classroom in a suburban school in northern California. The school serves an ethnically diverse, middle-income population. The school year runs from late August to mid-June. Daily class time is a half-day program of three hours and 20 minutes. Class size is 30 children ranging in age at the beginning of the school from 4.9 to 5.11 years.

The formal study took place in November and December of the 1990-91 school year. During the school year preceding the formal study, the author made twice-monthly informal observations of housekeeping play in preparation for the formal study. During these observations, the author would sit near the housekeeping area and take notes on the children's play behavior. Following the November-December formal study, the researcher resumed informal observations January through June of 1991. On occasion during both the pre- and post-observations, audio- and videotapes were made of children's play.

For the purposes of the formal study, six children (three female and three male) were randomly selected case study participants (see Steffey, 1992, for specific procedural details). Each participant was recorded on audio- and videotape while engaged in housekeeping play with three other children during regular playtime. The first 20 minutes of play were recorded, after which the child was asked to leave housekeeping and join the researcher in watching the videotape. While viewing the tape, the researcher asked the child open-ended questions to elicit interpretation and narration of play. These informant-interviews were recorded on audiotape.

The audio- and videotapes of play were transcribed to typescript. Typescripts served as the primary data source and were triangulated with written transcripts of informant-interview audiotapes and researcher field notes. Field notes had been taken before, during, and after play.

Triangulated data was analyzed and scored according to the Smilansky Scale for Evaluation of Dramatic and Sociodramatic Play (Smilansky & Shefatya, 1990) to determine the presence of the six elements.

For purposes of analysis, each 20-minute play period per child was divided into four five-minute intervals. Every five-minute interval was analyzed and scored separately for the presence of each element on a scale of 0-3, 0 representing not present and 3 representing highly elaborated. Scores were averaged across play periods, for each participant, to derive a mean score for each element.

Data analysis across 20-minute time periods indicates the presence of all six elements of sociodramatic play in the play behavior of each child. As represented in Table 1, the overall mean score of each element by participant ranged from 0.5, barely present, to 3.0, highly elaborated. Descriptions of the six elements follow.

1. Imitative role play. Imitation in role play is defined as taking on the role of someone other than oneself.

   In housekeeping, the children most often

Element	Participants					
	#1	#2	#3	#4	#5	#6
1. Role play	1.2	2.8	1.0	3.0	2.5	2.8
2. Make-believe with objects	1.2	2.8	1.8	3.0	2.3	2.8
3. Make-believe with actions and situations	1.5	2.8	1.0	2.5	2.3	2.5
4. Persistence	1.0	2.8	.5	3.0	2.8	2.8
5. Interaction	1.2	2.8	1.2	3.0	3.0	2.8
6. Verbalization	1.2	2.8	.5	3.0	3.0	2.5

Table 1: Overall mean score by element per participant over 20-minute play period
Rating scale: 0-3
Element is highly elaborated: Score 3
Element is present to a moderate degree: Score 2
Element is present to a limited degree: Score 1
Element is not evident: Score 0

*#1. Daniel, #2. Julie, #3. James, #4. Megan, #5. Jeff, #6. Kim

took the roles of immediate family members — father, mother, sister, brother, baby. On occasion, they became family pets. Roles were announced by the children as they entered the play area and, while roles might be renegotiated later, play begins within the first few minutes of entering the housekeeping area. As revealed through the informant interviews, the children always considered themselves to be in a role while physically within the boundaries of the housekeeping play area.

2. Make-believe with objects. Make-believe with objects is the representation of an object by another object, or through gestures or words.

On the whole, and probably because the children were surrounded with typical housekeeping play props, make-believe use of objects was of an imitative rather than an imaginative nature. Props were most often used in the manner in which they were intended. The children imitated behavior they had observed in the use of real objects. Imaginative use of props was minimally evident when brooms were once used as paint brushes, the refrigerator was used as a computer, and, in a pinch, the salt shaker became a second telephone.

3. Make-believe with actions and situations. Make-believe with actions and situations is defined as the representation of actions and situations through words or gestures.

The children's play tended to be composed of a series of pretend situations. Situations were loosely connected to a general theme or storyline. In some instances, the theme of the play came out of the situation. For example, the theme "moving to a new house" arose from a situation of the father and son painting the interior of a house. Typically, situations followed one upon another as in improvisational theater. In this case, painting the walls led to painting the door, which led to the paintbrush breaking and needing to be fixed, and so on.

Situations such as painting the house are actualized through pretend actions. Actions typically involve use of props, gestures, and words. In this case, the children used the kitchen brooms in combination with painting motions and talk about painting to signify the situation.

4. Persistence in role. Persistence is defined as a series of in-role activities enacted within the context of the play theme.

As previously mentioned, and although not always obvious to an observer, the children always considered themselves to be in role. Sometimes the role was highly developed and fully-elaborated. At other times, children assumed a role because that was the usual expectation at the housekeeping center and elaboration was kept to a minimum. Daniel presents an example of the full range of role persistence. In the first half of his play, Daniel uses words, actions and make-believe to expand on his role as the son. In the second half, he becomes frustrated in his attempt to change roles, the other children will not allow it, and he announces that he is no longer playing. He sits by himself at the kitchen table observing the other children. When Megan tries to set the table for a meal, Daniel creates a disturbance by methodically dropping the dishes on the floor. In the interview after play, Daniel explains that he was upset and did not want to continue playing. He stayed because "we have to stay in there." Dropping the dishes was prompted by a sense of frustration with the other children, yet during the interview, Daniel explained his behavior as playing the baby being angry with his parents.

5. Social interaction. Social interaction occurs when two or more children interact within the context of the play theme.

Play which is characterized by elements one through four is known as dramatic play. When the fifth element, social interaction, and the sixth element, verbal communication, are present, the play is sociodramatic. The children share in the pretense of the dramatic play through their actions and words. On the surface, in the November-December, 1990 study the children appear to be interacting as a group. Closer analysis reveals, however, that interactive behaviors most often occurred between pairs of children. This tendency to play in pairs will be more fully discussed in a later section of this paper.

6. Verbal communication. Verbal communication occurs when the children talk among themselves and the talk is related to the play.

Verbal communication occurred frequently both in and out of role. Out of role, the communication serves to inform about the play. When Megan instructs, "Pretend it was my birthday...," she has momentarily stepped out of her role in order to set up a play situation. In-role communication is part of the play as when Charlie says, "Mom, you always forget to sweep." While remaining in role, he explained why he was sweeping, reaffirmed Jenny as the mother and elaborated on the play situation.

Just as the children tended to interact in pairs, so too did they converse. Written transcripts of the children's conversations indicate a tendency to direct comments and responses to only one child at a time. Some children were able to engage in conversations on different subjects. For example, Megan carries on one conversation with Carlos about his running away from home. In between talking to Carlos, she talks with Jeff about the food she is preparing for him.

In conclusion, it appears that, for these six children, the elements of sociodramatic play associated with the development of skills and concepts underlying academic success are evident in kindergarten housekeeping play.

Part II

The formal study and pre- and post-observation data suggest the possibility of four other elements, or secondary characteristics, of sociodramatic play that are not as well understood as the six primary elements. These characteristics are:

1. Child-selected activity
2. Tendency to play in pairs
3. Pretense within pretense
4. Insider perspective

Methodology

These proposed characteristics of play began to emerge during the informal observations of 1989-90, were more thoroughly generated during an analysis of the data from the pre- and post-study observations, and a second analysis of the November-December, 1990 data.

The intent of the original study was to deter-mine if the six elements of sociodramatic play were evident in the housekeeping play of kindergarten children. The formal study in November of 1990 was undertaken to provide the data for this specific purpose. After the completion of the original study, it was decided to take a second look at the data from the perspective of a micro-ethnography. All of the data available regarding housekeeping play, from both informal and formal observations, was combined and treated as ethnographic material. Information contained in field notes, typescripts of audio- and videotapes, and transcripts of informant interviews were analyzed as ethnographic data (Fetterman, 1989). As such, categories for organizing and studying the data were generated from the data as opposed to being pre-determined before data collection.

1. Child-selected activity. As the work of Nancy King (1979) points out, the kindergarten child's definition of play rests on who selected the activity rather than how enjoyable it is. If the teacher chooses the activity for the child, it is work, no matter how pleasurable it may be.

   During the informal pre-study observations of 1989-90, the researcher began to sense that how a child comes to be at an activity not only determines the distinction between work and play but may also affect behavior. In the 1989-90 school year, the classroom teacher was following a procedure whereby the "special person" for the day automatically went to the housekeeping center during the activity period. The teacher assumed housekeeping to be a favored activity and wanted to provide equal time there for all children. The "special person" was to choose three other children to make up the housekeeping play group.

   During the twice-monthly observations in 1989-90, the researcher began to notice that the play behavior of the "special person" was often very unproductive and unfocused. It seemed to the researcher that in most cases, the child who was the "special person" either had no interest in housekeeping from the start or quickly lost interest. There was an understood rule in the classroom that children were to stay at the housekeeping center for the 40-minute play period. Since the "special person" could not officially leave, there was a tendency to go in and out of the center. The 1989-90 field notes and audio- and videotape typescripts contain numerous examples of children, particularly the "special person," coming and going from housekeeping. In almost every recorded observation, there were periods of time when the housekeeping center was vacant.

The 1989-90 notes and typescripts contain examples of inappropriate or threatening use of housekeeping props. Brooms being used as guns, bathroom behavior with dolls, playing chase, and using the iron on one another are examples. In a typical 10-minute period, the "special person" wandered in and out of the housekeeping center two times before finally stopping in the kitchen area. Without talking to the other children, he settled into the child-size rocker. One of the other children, who had been playing in the kitchen, mimicked throwing a cup of coffee at the "special person." The "special person" taunted, "You missed!"

Based on the 1989-90 observations, classroom procedures were changed for the 1990-91 year. Children decided whether to go to the housekeeping center. The records of play behavior for this year, including the formal November-December study and weekly spring post-study informal observations, are revealingly different: Children remain in the housekeeping center, engaged in play, and do not wander in and out. The housekeeping center is never vacant. Props are more often used in an appropriate manner and there are no instances of threatening behavior. Play behavior is focused and themes and situations are well-developed.

In the midst of such productive play, however, two instances stand out. These instances may be attributed to the fact that while children could choose to go in the housekeeping center, they were still supposed to stay for the entire play period. As previously mentioned in Part I, Daniel became upset when the other children would not let him change his role. He spent the remaining minutes at housekeeping dropping dishes on the floor. Megan, whose job was to pick up the dishes, implored, "Hey, stop it! Gimme that. Hey, stop it! You're making a mess,

Daniel. Stop. Okay, get out right now!" The problem was that Daniel did not feel free to leave. He remained in the housekeeping area and his behavior became disruptive to the play of the other children.

James presents another example of a child who remained in play at the housekeeping center even though he wanted to leave. He indicated in the informant interview that although he initially chose to enter play there, he quickly decided he would rather play with blocks. Staying at the housekeeping center, he spent most of his time watching other play elsewhere in the classroom. Although his behavior never became disruptive, James never quite synchronized his play with the others. For at least 10 minutes, the children talked about going to a ball before James suddenly asked, "What? A ball? A ball over here? It's all right with me, okay?" Without waiting for a response, he walked away.

2. Tendency to play in pairs.

It became apparent during transcribing of the audio- and videotapes that the participant's words and actions were most often directed at only one child. Frequently, the transcribed text read as a dialogue and series of interactions between only two children, the participant and a partner. When interaction with a third or fourth child occurred, it was typically brief, the participant quickly returning to the first partner.

This apparent tendency to play in pairs became even more obvious to the researcher in the spring of 1991. During weekly informal post-study observations, there were occasions when only three children instead of the usual four were in the playhouse. Frequently, although all three children were engaged in the same theme, one of the three children would appear to play a role peripheral to the other two children. One example comes from the first recorded observation of threesome play. On this occasion, Jenny, Marissa and Jennifer were at housekeeping. Upon entering housekeeping, Marissa and Jennifer immediately establish themselves in the kitchen area and begin meal preparation. Jenny goes to the kitchen area, takes a number of dishes, pots, and pans, and sets up her own kitchen in the bedroom. Jenny then engages the children at the block center in her play.

In a second example, the third child at play is Carlos. Carlos takes the role of the baby; the others are the mom and dad. The baby crawls around on the floor and is generally ignored. Carlos' role is ultimately eliminated when the parents decide they are not yet married and are going to have a wedding. Carlos tries to maintain his position by suggesting, "then pretend I came from an orphanage." He ultimately sits outside the housekeeping area waiting for the wedding to take place.

It may be that five-year-old children are just developing the ability to engage in shared pretense with peers as opposed to play with parents or older siblings and playmates. Young children may need to develop expertise while part of pairs before being able to include two or three others more directly in their make-believe.

3. Pretense within pretense. Pretense is the creation, understanding, and enacting of an "as if" situation. It appears that there can be pretend actions and situations within the "as if" situation.

There were instances throughout the 1989-90 year and the 1990-91 year, from both informal and formal observations, of occasions when the pretense seems to have this added layer of abstraction. An example from the 1989 field notes has Katie and John, among a group of four children, playing dog-owner and dog. John, as the dog, tells Katie to pretend that she had tied him up and he had run away and come back. Katie is to further pretend that she did not know he had run away. Children seem to be able to engage in pretense within their already existing pretense, a pretend-pretend.

Such pretense within pretense was most particularly exhibited on the occasions of threesome play in spring 1991. A rather prolonged example occurred with Stacey, Uyen, and Jennifer. Stacey and Uyen had dressed up to go to the theater. Jennifer was sitting in the rocking chair in the middle of the housekeeping area, talking on the telephone. Since the housekeeping center was to be the theater, the problem was, what to do with Jennifer? Stacey instructed Jennifer to pretend she was dreaming and that in her dream she goes to the theater and sees

Stacey and Uyen. The play goes on to have Stacey and Uyen go to the theater and return home to tell Jennifer, "We saw you at the theater saying, 'It's a dream. It's a dream.'"

Another example takes place in the previously-mentioned threesome play of Jenny, Marissa, and Jennifer. When Jenny tired of playing house with her neighbors at the block center, she attempted to play more directly with Marissa and Jennifer. The bedroom area became an attic as Jenny instructed Jennifer and Marissa, still playing together in the kitchen, to pretend she is their runaway daughter who is hiding in the attic. Further, she instructed them to pretend they called to her but she did not answer because she was not there.

The examples of pretense within pretense seemed more prevalent in the threesome play. Perhaps the challenge of playing as three, instead of in pairs, required an even greater depth of abstraction and pretense.

4. Insider's perspective.

In 1989, during an initial informal observation, it became evident to the researcher that only the players were really qualified to interpret the play. In a particular instance, one of the girls at play appeared to have become distracted as she leaned over a divider to watch the children at the block center. After play, when asked by the researcher about her behavior, she said she had been looking out the window at the neighbors. Obviously, or maybe not so obviously, intent of play behavior cannot be surmised by outside observation. Based on this experience, eliciting children's explanation and narration of play was built into both the formal and informal observations.

Most often, children's actions and talk during play make clear play behavior and intentions, as when Jeff and Charlie first planned and then "tracked" girls, pretending to use a refrigerator-turned-computer. Yet, when Jeff was later observed sweeping in the kitchen, it appeared that he had returned to the cooking play that preceded the "tracking" scenario. When asked during an interview why he was sweeping in the kitchen around the refrigerator, Jeff responded, "That's not a refrigerator." He made it clear that he was sweeping the dirt away from the computer target.

Sometimes the full understanding of play behavior is not even shared among all the children at play. Intent may be known only to an individual child. During an interview, Megan viewed a tape of herself at play and explained she had just returned from a day at work, that she was dressing up to go on a date, and was going to feed the baby again, and blamed herself for a disagreement between two of the other children. None of this was evident in conversations with the other children or from Megan's behavior.

Summary and Conclusion

There are six elements of play that are well-defined and accepted in the literature (Smilansky, 1968; Smilansky & Shefatya, 1990). According to the formal study described in this paper, these six elements appear to be present in the housekeeping play of six kindergarten children. Having determined the presence of well-known elements of play, a further analysis was undertaken to provide an even broader description of sociodramatic play. Data from informal observations undertaken pre- and post-study was combined with the data from the formal study and analyzed in the manner of a micro-ethnography. From this analysis, four additional elements of sociodramatic play appeared. These secondary characteristics are presented as suggestions for further study in response to the question, "What's going on here?"

References

Bateson, G. (1972). *Steps to an ecology of mind*. New York: Ballantine Books.

Fetterman, D. (1989). *Ethnography, step by step*. Newbury Park, Calif.: Sage Publications.

King, N. (1979). Play: The kindergartener's perspective. *Elementary School Journal, 80*, 81-87.

Parten, M. (1932). Social participation among preschool children. *Journal of Abnormal and Social Psychology, 27*, 243-262.

Piaget, J. (1954). *The construction of reality in the child*. New York: Basic Books.

Piaget, J. (1962). *Play, dreams and imitation in childhood*. New York: W. W. Norton and Co.

Smilansky, S. (1968). *The effects of sociodramatic play on disadvantaged children*. New York: Wiley.

Smilansky, S. & Shefatya, L. (1990). *Facilitating play: A medium for promoting cognitive, socio-emotional and academic development in young children*. Gaithersburg, Md.: Psychosocial and Educational Publications.

Steffey, M. S. (1992). <u>Evidence of sociodramatic play during kindergarten playtime</u>. Unpublished doctoral dissertation, University of San Francisco, California.

Vygotsky, L. (1962). *Thought and language*. Cambridge, Mass.: Massachusetts Institute of Technology Press.

M. STEPHANIE STEFFEY, ED.D. is a former classroom teacher now on the faculty in the Division of Teacher Education at San Jose State University in California.

Part IV
Chapter 12
Children's Play: Diagnostic Pictures

SUNNY DAVIDSON

For children, everywhere is a playground. A playground is not a place, but a space. Children experience space by using movement, all senses and imagination, each one in an individual and inimitable manner. Each person comes to realization of her own world by doing, thinking, enthusiastic exploration, creating a personal play experience.

Play cannot be defined in word, for a definition is confining. To define play would be a contradiction, because it cannot be confined within a verbal fence. Play is individual, spontaneous, open-minded. It is all-consuming, captivating, joyous. It is a combination of interest, curiosity, stimulation, problem-solving, and thinking. It is *not* competitive, directed, nor timed.

If adults would take the time and energy and knowledge to observe children at play, they would see more clearly the value of play. Play is not an afterthought. It is an inner thought. It is the way children learn about their world, their relationships, their inner beings, their image of self.

When adults are thus totally engaged, we define our activity as intense interest in a project, perhaps leading to accomplishment. If adults would watch and listen closely to children at play, they might relearn the joy of childhood. They might know more of the journey of experiences that it takes to make a child into an adult and think less of the goal to be accomplished. Childhood should be a journey ... not a race.

If adults could capture the joy of children's play, they could work more joyfully and play more freely.

These pictures are of children at play. Look openly at the hands, arms, legs and minds moving together. Experience the feelings of being alone and of discussing feelings with another person.

Look at the eyes — where the soul and inner person are visible. Enjoy, with each child at each developmental stage, the sheer pleasure of learning through play.

SUNNY DAVIDSON is director of a church-based child care program in Wichita Falls, Texas. KELLY QUINN is a photographer in Little Rock, Arkansas.

When bubbles are in the air, my fingers automatically open wide. I *need* to catch them.

I think I can ... I think I can ... but the security of holding to something stable is a safe bet.

Very close communion ... a circle of relationships ... some independent, some interdependent.

Learning to communicate through language. Learning to negotiate with hands and feet and hair and arms and mount and understanding.

Totally absorbed in the learning process through play ... alone and with others.

The more a child has the opportunity to try on another image, the more the self-image expands. Socio-dramatic play enhances a good self-image.

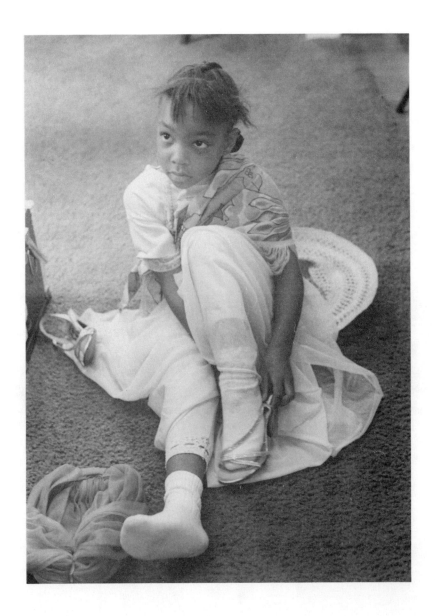

Looking at a garden during a pause in ball play.

In solitary play, the child is in charge of people, dinosaurs, scenario, time, sound, and action. It is his own world.

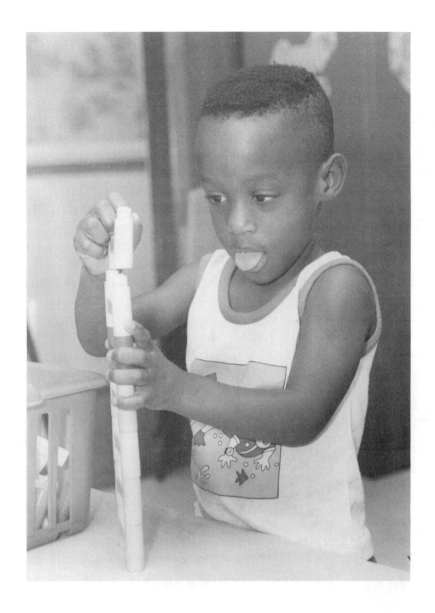

Part V
Children's Play: Anatomy of Parts

In this section, inventing games, having loose parts and selecting the right toy, producing movement structures, and integrating play with art education all add up to creative design implications that enhance children's play potential.

As children we all played games. According to **Castle** and **Wilson,** we not only replayed games previously played, we probably also invented unique new games known only to ourselves. The authors remind us of the developmental value of the game invention process. Creativity, culture, imitation and modeling, development of organizational skills, problem-solving, understanding rules and the decision-making process are all connected as the child invents games. Castle and Wilson make three suggestions to adults to encourage children to invent games: schedule ample time for play, provide interesting materials and equipment, and introduce group games that children like to play.

To have or not to have "loose parts" on your playground — that is the question posed by **Dempsy** and **Strickland**. They discuss this almost forgotten element of the play environment in terms of importance, types and functions, and those problems typically perceived by teachers, caretakers, and school administrators which invariably restrict the inclusion of loose parts on most playgrounds. What are loose parts? Why have loose parts? The authors tell us why playgrounds in educational settings must have loose parts. They conclude with four sound solutions for those wary of loose parts play.

We can easily agree that toys are a part of children's play, but agreeing on what toys are appropriate is another matter. Miller attacks this issue with vigor, stating that adults have a great responsbility to provide toys that will help facilitate, not hinder, learning and development. A list of 15 criteria that can help child care providers and parents choose appropriate toys is provided.

Guilfoil's "Creating Urban Designs" is an outgrowth of the 1990 Playful City Conference at Stanford University. Her premise is that educating youth to participate in urban design can lead to more playful experiences and responsible roles in childhood and adulthood. Guilfoil aptly describes the relationship of art and play and how art education can provide needed experiences by involving youth in real and simulated urban design decisions and activities as part of art classes.

Since there had been little research done to determine or suggest physical education activities that are developmentally appropriate for three- and four-year-old children, **Clements** developed a preschool physical education network to facilitate communication between eight New York area preschool and nursery schools that were desiring cooperative play activities. The overall goal of this interdisciplinary network has been to exchange information related to childhood social development and movement theories in hopes of selecting or creating developmentally appropriate physical education activity for this age. Clements discusses the primary content of this program, "Movement Structures," which refers to the child's use of body parts to produce developmentally appropriate and identifiable shapes, objects, and traveling actions.

Chapter 13
Creativity through Children's Invented Games

KATHRYN CASTLE
ELAINE WILSON

Children of all ages play games. Even infants will spontaneously initiate simple games with adults. Children not only replay games they have previously played, they also invent unique games known only to themselves. Inventing games gives children an opportunity to construct knowledge of games and social conventions such as rules and to express what they are learning in classrooms and in life. When children have a chance to invent games at school and to play according to their understanding of rules, their social, cognitive, and moral development is enhanced (Kamii & DeVries, 1980; DeVries & Kohlberg, 1987; DeVries, Reese-Learned, & Morgan, 1991). Children exercise thinking, social, verbal, and physical skills, and creativity within the meaningful context of inventing a game.

It may seem that creativity in children suffers if they spend many hours watching television, playing video games, or playing adult-directed sports. But if you observe children in child-initiated play and listen closely, you will see that creativity is very much alive in children's invented games.

Children begin inventing simple games in infancy to try out their ideas about how the world works (Maxwell, 1983). Some kinds of play and games are universal (Grunfeld, 1982). Games of chase, follow the leader, tug of war, hopscotch, jump rope, hoops, kickball, darts, and marbles, are found in most cultures. These games have developed simultaneiously in separate cultures and are passed from one generation to another.

Children learn games by watching and playing with other children and adults. They play to be near other children, to exercise their bodies

and practice emerging physical skills, and to have fun. Although children learn such things as rules, number relationships, vocabulary, and social customs through games, they play primarily for fun. They most enjoy the games which they invent themselves and games which involve movement such as running, batting, aiming, throwing, and catching. Child-initiated play of this type promotes their physical, cognitive, and social-moral development. When they invent games, children are in control. They decide the type of game, the equipment needed, and the rules to follow. Thus, this activity promotes their autonomy and ability to make decisions (Kamii and Joseph, 1989).

Inventing games helps children develop organizational skills needed to put plans into action. Through teaching the game to others, playing the games, and modifying the game to improve it, children develop problem-solving skills. This type of play promotes cooperation with others, taking turns, and seeing the situation from another's perspective. When conflicts occur, children can discuss the problem from everyone's viewpoint and decide on a mutually acceptable solution. Such constructive conflict resolution increases children's abilities to negotiate and compromise and reduces their egocentrism (Tudge and Caruso, 1988).

Inventing rules for games promotes a deeper understanding of why rules are of benefit to the majority of those playing (Castle, 1990). Young children's ideas about rules are different from the adult perspective. Very young children tend to view rules as imposed externally by authority figures (Piaget, 1965). They do not yet comprehend and experience how common rules make the game competitive. They play the game egocentrically, not recognizing that other children are playing by different rules. When left alone to play according to their understanding, preschoolers become more assertive and creative in making rules. Children who view themselves as being able to make better rules are more likely to make effective decisions.

Even though they may not know the rules, preschool-age children will enter the games of older children who look like they are having fun. Younger children will imitate the actions of older children and may play out of turn or interfere with the game sequence. Older children will often tolerate such behavior and try to explain to the young ones why the behavior interferes with the game. Sometimes older children take over and play the younger child's turn while the younger child watches.

Once children become aware that established games have specific rules (about six to seven years of age), they attempt to impose the rules on others. Rules take on an external existence and authority. Gradually (by about eight or nine years of age), children develop the idea that game rules can be modified or replaced through mutual agreement. Children in constructivist programs that promote child-initiated game-playing are more likely to express ownership of classroom rules and see themselves as creators of rules (DeVries, Reese-Learned, and Morgan, 1991). Through inventing rules for games, children come to feel they have an important role in the democratic process. They will want to invent games and rules that others find challenging and enjoyable. They can adopt rules for competitive or cooperative strategies.

Suggestions for Practice

Adults can encourage children to invent games by scheduling ample time for play, providing interesting materials and equipment, introducing group games that children like to play, and playing with children in their games. The following ideas have been tried successfully by early childhood teachers.

Respect Play

Play is valued and playing should not be used as a reward or punishment. Play integrates the curriculum areas. Play is not a reward for doing boring work. Play is the way children learn and cope. Play comes first.

Allow Enough Time

Long periods of time (at least 30 minutes) support sustained interest in the development of ideas. When play is brief, children cannot develop and expand on their game ideas and are less likely to have time to modify their games and teach them to others. The creative process takes time and suffers when it is rushed.

Encourage Games

Children should be free to play or leave a game. Suggesting, not forcing, popular games and playing the games with children shows that you are interested in their activities. As an equal participant, you will be able to question rule infractions without seeming like an enforcer of rules. Encouraging children to invent their own games shows that you value their ideas.

Resist Temptations to Impose Adult Rules

Children play according to their understanding of rules, which may be different from an adult's view. Children may choose to modify existing rules or make up new ones. This activity promotes taking perspective and learning to negotiate. Give children opportunities to modify rules. Then they will see that they have an important role to play in rule-making and that their thinking counts.

Promote Constructive Conflict Resolution

Conflicts are inevitable and can be meaningful learning experiences when children solve them. Even two-year-olds can become great negotiators (McCracken, 1987). When children settle disputes, such as disagreements over who will have the next turn, they learn to accommodate others' ideas about how to play. Constructive conflict resolution leads to increased cooperation and mutual enjoyment in social interactions. Adults can facilitate constructive conflict resolution by pointing out the ideas and needs of others and by suggesting choices where there is an impasse. Of course, adults need to intervene when health or safety are at risk. Orlick (1978) observed that children who invented games never created games of hitting each other, games in which numbers of children were inactive, or games where children would be eliminated.

Focus on Cooperation, not Winning

Races, "Olympics," ribbons, awards, and comparisons of abilities are examples of impositions of adult standards on children. Children often play for the fun of the activity and not to win or beat someone else. Children may decide to make a game competitive. Child-initiated competition is inevitable but different from adult-imposed competition. As long as it does not become destructive or an end in itself, child-initiated competition may add an element of interest and challenge to a game. Adults can introduce cooperative group games and help children convert competitive games to cooperative ones.

There are three different ways of playing games. In fact, these are ways to approach most tasks. People function best when they are capable of all three styles. Then they can select the behavior which is most appropriate to each situation.

1. Competition: One maximizes own gain, minimizes others' gain.
2. Cooperation: One maximizes own gain along with others' gain.
3. Individualistic: One maximizes own gain with no impact on others' gain (Johnson & Johnson, 1991).

Adults can encourage children to play games in all three ways. Children can compare their feelings, success, and enjoyment under each condition. For example, a teacher might ask, "How can you play the games so you both win?" or "Now try the game working together and helping each other in your games."

When younger children do not understand strategy or see the effect of their moves on others' success, adults might ask, "What do you do to finish the game?" or ask "What makes a player win or lose?" The children's answers and their play behavior reveal whether they are playing competitively.

Individualistic behavior may involve practice alone, competition with one's self, or parallel game playing. These activities help preschoolers adapt and deal with the stress of competition as they learn how to play games.

Allow Extended Game Set-ups

Children may construct an obstacle course or game apparatus with materials or equipment. If they would like to continue playing the next day, allow the structure to stand undisturbed if possible. When children can return to a popular game, their ideas of game-playing and inventing can become more complex. They learn that some projects are ongoing and develop a sense of accomplishment for work in progress.

Provide a Great Variety of Open-ended Materials.

A variety of materials such as wood, nails, boxes, containers, tape, cardboard cylinders, string, chalk, and balls of various shapes and sizes promotes game invention (Castle, 1990). Provide table, work benches, and concrete surfaces for work areas. Adults should supervise construction with hammers, nails, and other tools.

Record Individual Progress

Children's progress in play and game invention can be recorded and shared with parents to show how much they have grown during the year. Teachers can shoot quick photographs of invented games, keep anecdotal records of activities, and interview children about what they have learned. They can discuss these experiences in parent conferences and program descriptions. Other adults can learn much by observing children as they invent and play games. They will see that child's play is not wasted time.

Inventing games is a way for children to develop in all areas, especially in creative expression and problem-solving. Children develop satisfaction and a sense of competence as they create games which others enjoy and want to play again and again.

References

Castle, K. (1990, Winter). Children's invented games. *Childhood* Education, *67*(2), 82-85.

DeVries, R., & Kohlberg, L. (1987). *Programs for early education.* New York: Longman.

DeVries, R., Reese-Learned, H., & Morgan, P. (1991). Sociomoral development in direct-instruction, eclectic, and constructivist kindergartens: A study of children's enacted interpersonal understanding. *Early Childhood Research Quarterly, 6*(4), 473-511.

Grunfeld, F. (1982). *Games of the world.* Swiss Committee for UNICEF, New York: Plenary Publications.

Johnson, D. & Johnson, R. (1991). *Learning together and alone: Cooperative competitive and individualistic learning.* 3rd Ed. Englewood Cliffs, NJ: Prentice Hall.

Kamii, C., & DeVries, R. (1980). *Group games.* Washington, DC: National Association for the Education of Young Children.

Kamii, C., & Joseph, L. (1989). *Young children continue to reinvent arithmetic, 2nd grade.* New York: Teacher's College Press.

Maxwell, W. (1983). Games children play. *Educational Leadership, 40*(6), 38-41.

McCracken, J. (1987). *Play is fundamental.* Washington, D.C.: National Association for the Education of Young Children.

Orlick, T. (1978). *The cooperative sports & games book; Challenge without competition.* New York: Pantheon Books.

Piaget, J. (1965). *The moral judgment of the child.* New York: Free Press.

Tudge, J. & Caruso, D. (1988). Cooperative problem solving in the classroom: Enhancing young children's cognitive development. *Young Children, 44*(1), 46-52.

KATHRYN CASTLE, ED.D., is a professor of curriculum and instruction at Oklahoma State University. ELAINE WILSON, PH.D., is an associate professor of Family Relations and Child Development at Oklahoma State University and a parenting specialist for the Cooperative Extension Service.

Chapter 14
The "Why"s Have It!
Why and Why Not to Include Loose Parts on the Playground

JIM DEMPSEY
ERIC STRICKLAND

Recent interest in improving American playgrounds has resulted in an explosion of activity (Dempsey and Frost, 1993) as play equipment manufacturers seek to introduce more developmentally appropriate equipment and to comply with new federal guidelines (U.S.C.P.S.C., 1991). This is necessary given the deplorable state of playgrounds in America (Wortham and Frost, 1990; Bruya and Langendorfer, 1988). Improvements should be made to increase both safety and educational value. The outdoor play environment can and should be seen as a rich opportunity for learning, one which has unique advantages in comparison to the indoor environment (Frost and Dempsey, 1991).

When children play on a playground, they interact with an environment which may include portable items, stationary play equipment, other people, and natural features such as grass, sand, or trees. Designers of outdoor play environments often include stationary play equipment but neglect these other aspects of this environment. In this paper we will address one of the forgotten elements of the play environments: portable items or "loose parts." We will discuss the importance of loose parts, different types of loose parts and their functions, and perceived problems which restrict the inclusion of loose parts by many playground "overseers" (teachers, caregivers, school administrators).

Loose parts are easily moved materials which may be used by children while playing. They may be "found" materials such as sticks, leaves, or rocks, or they may be provided materials like boxes, parachutes or tricycles. Playgrounds in educational settings must have loose parts in order to be complete. Why loose parts? There are several reasons.

Reasons to Include Loose Parts on Playgrounds
1. Loose parts encourage children to manipulate their environment.

Current developmental theory emphasizes the need for the child to manipulate his environment, to experiment, and to interact with materials in order to learn (Piaget, 1963). Environments rich in loose parts allow extensive manipulation of the environment and much experimentation. Manipulation of materials through play is important in problem-solving (Sylva, 1977), and creativity (Dansky, 1980). Stationary equipment restricts the ways children can manipulate the environment, thereby restricting opportunities for creativity and problem-solving. A reliance on fixed equipment in the playground sends a subtle but powerful message to the child: "What you have to offer in creating this environment does not count." Such a message runs counter to the goal of helping children learn to make choices. Just as allowing children to help make rules for behavior gives them an investment in those rules, allowing children to have a part in creating their environment through daily interaction with loose parts gives children an investment in their learning environment.

2. Children choose playground equipment based on the amount of movement the equipment affords and the amount of variability it provides (Strickland, 1979).

This is consistent with current theories of arousal seeking as a motivator of play (Ellis, 1973, 1970) and is a valid reason to include loose parts on the playground. Nicholson (1971) pointed to this in her theory of loose parts: "In any environment, both the degree of inventiveness and the possibility of discovery, are directly proportional to the number and kind of variables in it" (p. 30). Loose parts present many variables for the child to experience as she chooses the way to organize or use the loose parts materials; she may choose to build a tall or short structure, to place it here or there, to mix in other materials, or to use the material as something other than its apparent use. The mental transformation of an L-shaped stick to a gun (though we might discourage it, usually unsuccessfully, on the basis of its violent theme) indicates a child's involvement in dramatic play. Other writers have pointed to the popularity of loose parts among children at play (Moore, 1974; Allen, 1968). Because children prefer loose parts to fixed equipment, designers should respect these preferences.

3. Loose parts provide children with age-appropriate materials because each age group uses the materials in different ways peculiar to and appropriate for that group.

Children use construction materials in different ways as they get older. For example, three-year-olds may build large corral-like enclosures with large hollow blocks, while four-year-olds using the same blocks may build towers. The materials provide age-appropriate play opportunities in either case in ways that fixed equipment cannot. In a study of play equipment preferences, Frost and Strickland (1985) found that loose parts were popular with children across kindergarten, first, and second grade. The flexibility of loose parts materials in appealing to and serving the needs of this age range makes the expenditure of funds for these materials a wise investment. Administrators and owners of early childhood programs can make their budgets go farther by purchasing materials that can be used by different ages.

4. Loose parts inject novelty into the play environment, which is important in maintaining cognitively high levels of play such as symbolic play (Dodge and Frost, 1986; Griffing, 1983).

When children have exhausted the possibilities of one arrangement of loose parts, they rearrange the materials for some new game or purpose. This maintains interest and gives children the ability to create the individually-appropriate level of arousal and interest. Fixed

equipment by its nature will become less novel more quickly than loose parts. Novelty can be increased by rotating in and out of the play environment a wide variety of materials.

5. Loose parts promote a wide variety of play behaviors.

They encourage exercise play as children lift, move, and stack materials. They encourage dramatic play as children build houses or use cups and sand to play tea party. They encourage construction play as children plan and create a new structure. Loose parts are involved in many games with rules, such as follow-the-leader, obstacle course, and various ball games. Loose parts provide opportunities for varied levels of social play. Toddlers sit together and play with sand toys in examples of parallel play while preschoolers create models of farms or cities and engage in cooperative dramatic play with those same sandtoys. Large blocks or boxes which may be too heavy or cumbersome for one child to move encourage cooperative effort.

Functions and Types of Loose Parts

Loose parts serve a variety of functions. As a part of the early childhood curriculum, they extend the indoor learning environment to the outdoors. Math skills are practiced and math concepts are inculcated as children manipulate small unit blocks, large blocks made of foam or cardboard, or large commercially made plastic interlocking blocks. Many ball games involve counting, sequencing, and one-to-one correspondence. Buckets, measuring cups, sand, water, sundials, and measuring tapes may be used to reinforce mathematical principles.

Physical science concepts are learned as children experiment with stacking materials. Boards and small cars and balls for experimentation with inclines, real tools and soft lumber, wind chimes, windmills, and color wheels all give opportunity for learning about physical science. Ample facilities for water play outdoors are crucial for learning about volume and the properties of fluids. Water tables, water troughs, buckets, cups, buckets with holes in varying places and sizes, clear plastic tubes, water wheel toys, brushes, straws, and sponges are some possibilities for this area.

Because loose parts construction play often requires a great deal of room, and because many of the materials are large, children learn social skills through group efforts. Large cardboard boxes such as appliance boxes encourage social play. Having numerous small sandbox toys allows toddlers to engage in parallel play.

Loose parts should be provided to encourage dramatic play in the outdoor environment. Prop boxes for theme-specific dramatic play can be prepared using materials especially suited for the rigors and weathering of outdoor use. Dress-up clothes used in the outdoor environment will need to be cleaned more often or made from the most expendable of materials. Almost anything that is used indoors can be adapted and replicated for the outdoor environment. Since tricycles and other wheeled vehicles are typically used outdoors, children can dramatize a number of transportation themes suited to the playground and supported by loose parts. Lengths of garden hose and a few firemen's hats, large boxes painted white with a red cross plus nurses' hats and doctors' paraphernalia, and scaled-down traffic signs can encourage specific themes of play in conjunction with wheeled vehicles. Cooking utensils available near the sandbox, and combined with a nearby playhouse, all form a recipe for rich domestic theme play.

Objections to Loose Parts Play: The "Why Nots"

The reasons for failing to provide for loose parts play are many and varied, ranging from "the playground will look messy" to "children don't have time for that at our school." The net effect is the same regardless of the excuse or reason: Children are robbed of a very valuable form of play. Perhaps the best way to approach the problem concerning the failure to provide for loose parts construction is to examine the reasons one at a time.

"All these kids need is a climber and slide for exercise."

Perhaps one of the greatest stumbling blocks to loose parts construction play is the general lack of knowledge about the importance of play itself. The role of play in development has been well researched and documented (Rubin, Fein,

and Vandenberg, 1983). Although a thorough discussion of play is impractical here, a brief mention of Piaget's (1962) work and Smilansky's (1968) work is appropriate. According to Piaget and Smilansky, children engage in four kinds of cognitively categorized play: exercise/functional, sociodramatic, construction play, and games with rules. Each form of play makes its own contributions to cognitive development, yet they all work together for the total growth of the individual. In fact, physical, social, and emotional development, as well as cognitive development, all are rooted in play behavior. To suppress one form of play may have a negative impact on the optimum development of the individual.

Another aspect of the issue concerning a lack of knowledge about play relates to the age-old dichotomy between work and play. Although it is probably more productive to consider the two as being on a continuum with play lapsing into work (the Dallas Cowboys play (work?) football) and work lapsing into play (One of the authors plays at woodworking), we rarely view work and play in a continuum, particularly where school settings are concerned. Instead, work is considered good and productive; play, frivolous and nonproductive. In school, work is equated with learning; play with not learning. Therefore, play is viewed as antithetical to learning. Such remarks as "I send my child to school to learn not play" reflect this attitude.

Construction play, however, conveniently blurs the distinction between work and play and between play and learning. Children labor diligently during play period to build a fort in which they can play. Children work to make an obstacle course which evolves into more complex arrangements as they use it. Children tear down and build up as part of their play. The process and the product easily merge. Furthermore, both process and product enhance and support learning, problem-solving, and social interaction. Work, play, and learning thus intermingle.

"Loose parts make the area so messy!"

A second issue which frequently mitigates against construction play is the concern for order.

Construction play materials by their very nature are not rigidly structured and well-defined as are ball game areas and exercise equipment (climbing bars, swings, etc.). Rather, construction play materials receive their structure during the process as children use the material. Consequently, the play itself, as well as the material to support such play, is not as neat and well-ordered as static equipment or the play which usually occurs on such equipment. In playground planning sessions, parents frequently express the notion that loose parts construction play "will look messy" or "might offend the neighborhood residents." Certainly, public relations must be maintained, but not at the expense of enriched learning activities for children. A loose parts construction area need not be trashy to have play value. Neatly painted and carefully-constructed props for loose parts play can be made by parents at minimal cost and may include boxes, planks, ramps, stools, and other materials. Several innovative commercial materials are available from vendors.

"Won't kids get hurt on this rickety old stuff?"

Often parent groups and administrators express a concern for children's safety. Loose parts construction is often viewed as a potentially hazardous activity for children. Two problems seem to generate most of the concern in this area: the use of tools and the height of equipment. Parents and teachers often mistakenly believe that woodworking tools are necessary in a loose parts construction area. In fact, they are not necessary since the construction can involve nonpermanent stacking and juxtaposing of pieces, requiring no tools or nails.

The second concern, that of height, seems to be misplaced. On almost any playground — particularly at public schools — one can see children who are too small for the height of the equipment they are using. The problem is compounded when unnecessary height is combined with a lack of adequate resilient surfaces below the equipment, yet these height-related problems often cause little concern. The authors do not wish to suggest that stacked objects falling on children are no cause for concern, but only that there are easy ways to deal with this concern and that other safety hazards are more

problematic on most playgrounds. (See U.S. Consumer Product Safety Commission Report, 1991). Also, playgrounds that are "too safe" or lack challenge, variety and novelty become inviting places for horseplay as children seek to create challenges, such as by walking on swingbeams as though they are balance beams.

"Who's going to take care of this stuff?"

Another frequently-cited excuse for failing to provide for loose parts construction play is the concern over maintenance. Parents and administrators are reluctant to provide for the maintenance of such items and the replacement of such items over time. Again, this concern seems misplaced. The belief that a rigid, metal fixed-position playground requires little or no maintenance is a false assumption that leads to many problems and injuries on playgrounds. Even metal equipment must be repaired and maintained, particularly if it is subjected to heavy use. To argue that not having construction play eliminates the need for maintenance is easily contradicted by a visit to local school playgrounds, where broken stationary equipment can be found easily.

Related to the issue of maintenance is the concern about disappearing play materials. Certainly, unattended loose parts on playgrounds—particularly in isolated or high-crime areas — will disappear. However, the fear that something might get stolen is no more an adequate reason for failing to provide for loose parts play than it is for failing to provide books. Solutions are available to eliminate the problem of theft.

Another issue concerning maintenance relates to who is responsible for cleaning up the loose parts area at the end of the day. Teachers often express this concern, fearing that it will become their responsibility. Certainly this is a valid concern, but not a sufficient reason to cheat children of productive play opportunities. Just as children learn responsibility for the indoor environment, they can learn such responsibility where the outdoor environment is concerned.

Although the above concerns are probably not the only ones which argue against the provision of loose parts construction play, they seem to be the ones which most often succeed in eliminating such play. Examining each one more closely serves to point out that they are probably more in the nature of excuses than reasons. The concerns, though legitimate, are not insurmountable. Often, minor adjustments are all that are needed. The section which follows offers some appropriate solutions to the problems.

The Solutions

Knowledge about Play

Certainly, the information about the relationship of play and children's total development should be part and parcel of every teacher's, parent's, and administrator's knowledge. Refresher courses on development, inservice sessions on play and playgrounds, parent meeting programs concerning play, and professional journals are all sources of knowledge concerning play.

School district administrators must become informed about play and its contribution to development and then make concerted efforts to communicate this to school personnel and to parents. The directors of physical education should be an integral part of this effort. Consultants, playground development specialists, and literature on play can serve as sources of information for school personnel as well as parents.

Order

School districts and administrators do have to be concerned with the appearance of school grounds. Carried to an extreme, however, this concern would convince us that the tidiest school would be one that never allowed children on the grounds! A loose parts construction area need not be messy or trashy. As suggested earlier, high-quality, brightly-colored construction materials can add aesthetic appeal to loose parts construction areas. Storage facilities for the materials when not in use can keep an area from looking messy. In addition, "a place for every thing" encourages responsibility among children.

Beyond attention to the nature of the materials and provision for storage, the loose parts construction area should be designed with aesthetics in mind. Wooden screens or shrubbery can effectively reduce passerby visibility into the loose parts area. (Care should be taken, however, not to restrict the teachers' and playground supervisors' view of the area.)

Safety

Aside from the most obvious deterrent to problems — carefully-designed and consistently-enforced guidelines on the heights of loose parts construction — other things can be done to assure safety. Carefully-maintained material is less likely to cause injury. Boards should be sanded; material checked for wear, and other such steps taken to keep material safe. Controlling the number of children in the area and restricting occupancy to children of the same approximate size and physical skill can help assure the safe use of these materials. Providing a variety of materials to make sure smaller children have access to easily-manipulated material also can increase safety. An adequate supply of materials can prevent arguments, which may result in safer play. Separation of loose parts play areas from fall zones is essential.

Maintenance

No playground is maintenance-free. Consequently, steps as described above are necessary to assure that the loose parts materials are kept in good condition. Beyond that, adequate storage can reduce the deterioration of materials due to overexposure to weather and can also reduce the amount of material that is lost due to theft. Storage can be provided in separate freestanding buildings, inside the school building, or in locked, fenced storage areas.

The physical appearance of the area can be enhanced in two ways. First, daily maintenance should be provided by the users of the area. Children can learn responsibility for picking up and cleaning up the area. Where necessary, a "playground patrol" as an honor guard can be appointed to assure that daily clean-up is done.

Second, additional maintenance is periodically required. Parent-teacher groups, working with children, can plan occasional workdays to repair and maintain the loose parts. Certainly, this type of family involvement might appeal to parents who cannot be available during the school day.

Conclusion

Just as the previously-mentioned concerns may not be the only ones related to loose parts construction play, the above suggestions do not exhaust the possible solutions to the problems. However, one thing remains clear: Loose parts play makes a vital contribution to children's development. It can be provided with a careful, reasonable effort by administrators, teachers, and families. To accept excuses denies children opportunities to play in meaningful, productive, and exciting ways.

References

Allen, M. (1968). Planning for play. Cambridge, Mass.: Massachusetts Institute of Technology Press.

Bruya, L. D. & Langendorfer, S. J. (Eds.). (1988). *Where our children play: Elementary school playground equipment.* Reston, Va.: American Alliance for Health, Physical Education, Recreation and Dance.

Dansky, J. L. (1980). Make-believe: A mediator of the relationship between play and associative fluency. *Child Development, 51,* 576-579.

Dempsey, J. D. & J. L. Frost. (1993). Play setting in early childhood eduation. In B. Spodek (Ed.), Handbook of *research on the education of young children.* New York: Macmillan, 307-323.

Dodge, M. K. & Frost, J. L. (1986). Children's dramatic play: Influence of thematic and nonthematic settings. *Childhood Education, 63,* 166-170.

Ellis, M. J. (1973).] *Why people play.* Englewood Cliffs, N.J.: Prentice Hall, Inc.

Frost, J. L. & Dempsey, J. D. (1991). Playgrounds for infants, toddlers, and preschoolers. In B. Brizzolara (Ed.), *Parenting education for school-age parents.* Lubbock, Texas: Home Economics Curriculum Center, Texas Tech University.

Frost, J. L. & Strickland, E. (1985). Equipment choices of young children during free play. In J. L. Frost & S. Sunderlin (Eds.), *When children play.* Wheaton, Md.: Associaion for Childhood Education International, 93-102.

Griffing, P. (1983). Encouraging dramatic play in early childhood. *Young Children, 38,* 13-22.

Moore, R. C. (1974). Anarchy zone: Kids' needs and school yards. *School Review, 82,* 621-645.

Nicholson, S. (1971). How not to cheat children: The theory of loose parts. *Landscape Architecture, 62,* 30-35.

Piaget, J. (1962). *Play, dreams and imitation in childhood.* New York: Norton.

Piaget, J. (1963). *The origins of intelligence in children.* New York: Norton.

Rubin, K., Fein, G., & Vandenberg, B. (1983). Play. In E. M. Hetherington (Ed.), *Handbook of child psychology: Socialization, personality, and social development, Vol. IV,* New York: Wiley, 693-774.

Smilansky, S. (1968). *The effects of sociodramatic play on disadvantaged preschool children.* New York: Wiley.

Strickland, E. V. (1979). Free play behaviors and equipment choices of third grade children in contrasting play environments. Unpublished doctoral dissertation, The University of Texas at Austin.

Sylva, K. (1977). Play and learning. In B. Tizard & D. Harvey (Eds.), *Biology of play.* London: Heinemann.

U.S. Consumer Product Safety Commission. (1991). *Handbook for public playground safety.* Washington, D.C.: U.S. Government Printing Office.

Wortham, S. C. & Frost, J. L. (Eds.) (1990). *Playgrounds for young children: National survey and perspectives.* Reston, Va.: American Alliance for Health, Physical Education, Recreation and Dance.

JIM DEMPSEY, PH.D.., is senior vice president of Grounds for Play, Inc., an Arlington, Texas firm which plans, manufactures, and installs outdoor play environments. His most recent design work has been in creating play environments which encourage full participation by physically challenged children. ERIC STRICKLAND, PH.D., was associate professor of elementary education at the University of Texas at Arlington. He is now president and chief executive officer of Grounds for Play, Inc., a firm which he founded in 1983. He has designed hundreds of children's play environments at schools, churches, hospitals, and parks.

Chapter 15
Choosing Appropriate Toys for Young Children

Linda G. Miller

The current play crisis in the United States is real and extends far beyond the dearth of opportunities for good open-ended outdoor play. Despite the numerous toys which children may have available to them both in their homes and in child care settings, many of the toy choices made for them are inappropriate and even dangerous. Because play is an essential element in child development, adults have a great responsibility to provide toys that will help facilitate, not hinder, learning and development.

When asked to recall childhood play, adults most often mention extended periods of free play involving choices, open-ended possibilities, and play unemcumbered by constant adult intervention. Clearly, these are not opportunities which most children enjoy today. Likewise, when asked to recall childhood toys, adults most often remember toys that supported very open-ended play, that kept their attention for long periods, and that lasted for years, perhaps even surviving to their adulthood — a favorite doll, building blocks, etc. Again, these types of toys are not those primarily being chosen by adults for children today.

Currently, children are being targeted not only by the traditional advertisements and commercials, but even more strongly by movies and network television programming. Increasingly, movies and television programs come with toys attached, and vice-versa. Timing is crucial, as the International Toy Fair in New York in January introduces to retailers toys which will be available to consumers during the high sales period that culminates the following Christmas. Most toys are never intended for marketing beyond a three-year period. During the first year, marketing is intense and the demand may exceed supply. During the second year, market-

ing is reduced and piggy-backs on demand of the previous year. During the third year, marketing is practially nonexistent and production shrinks tremendously. For most toys for which significant marketing occurs, a three-year life is the best-case scenario. The desire for immediate gratification in the form of sales drives the marketing strategy.

Consumerism is present not only in the short-lived marketing and availability of toys, but also in the quality of toys. They are not intended to last; quite literally, they are consumed — used up, presumably so that other toys can be bought to replace them. This same disposable-toy mentality is evident in the give-away toys available with many carry-out meals. Like their retail counterparts, these toys often are of poor quality and are simply thrown away when broken. No provision is made for repair, and like so many other items, the toys are discarded — not even recycled. Toys of this type communicate to children that resources are unlimited and that a *toss-away society* is fine.

The quality of the toy is very important, but the developmental appropriateness of the toy is, too. Toys chosen for children need to be appropriate for their ages and development. When a toy can be approached at a number of different levels and with open-ended results, a child is better able to experience a feeling of success; self-esteem is enhanced, and the time in which the child engages in play increases. Recommended ages on toy packages often have little if anything to do with the age or developmental level at which the toys are appropriate. The printed age recommendations often dupe the consumer into thinking that appropriate toy choices are easy and that some benevolent force is watching over and protecting chidren. This simply is not the case.

Even when recommended age designations

are appropriate, the consumer may misunderstand the designations or be tempted to ignore them. What parent hasn't thought that his very advanced two-year-old could easily handle a toy designated for older children? The parent may not suspect that small parts that a two-year-old may aspirate determined the older age recommendation instead of the level of a child's cognitive development.

In addition to concern for small parts contained in toys, adults need to be aware of the size of parts which may result from a break. Sharp edges, projectiles (eye danger), and plastic wrap (breathing hazard) are just a few other safety concerns. (Choke testers, available from many toy and educational supplies distributors, can determine if toy parts are small enough to cause a child to choke.)

The following criteria should be considered in any toy selection:

1. The toy is developmentally appropriate.
   •Challenging but not frustrating
   •Appropriate level of complexity

2. Toy can be approached from a variety of levels
   •Variety of developmental stages addressed
   •Lack of "functional fixedness"

3. Toy is safe for intended age group
   •Passes choke test (for infants through three-year-olds)
   •No sharp edges
   •No danger of suffocation
   •Eye danger considered

4. Toy is durable and intended for extended use
   •Will not soon break or become useless
   •Has play value for more than a few weeks or months

5. Toy is appealing to children
   •Color, shape, style best for age

6. Toy is appropriate for intended use at home or child care center
   •Size appropriate for available space
   •Can work for small or large numbers of children
   •Durable enough for expected use

7. Toy is appropriate for both indoor and outdoor use
   •Flexibility offers increased play value
   •Waterproof or easy to clean

8. Play opportunities are open-ended
   •Stimulates divergent thinking
   •More than one right answer or method of use

9. Toy is multicultural
   •Will contribute to variety of ethnic groups represented by toys
   •Is free of stereotypes (e.g., teepee for Native Americans)

10. Toy is free of sex stereotypes
    •Usable by both boys and girls
    •Colors don't dictate use by single sex
    •Does not dictate a certain role

11. Toy is nonviolent in nature
    •Weapons not included
    •Aggression not encouraged
    •Character does not represent violence

12. Toy is a result of responsible use of resources
    •Not disposable
    •Toy and packing are recycled or recyclable

13. Price of toy reflects its value
    •Resulting play and durability are worth the investment

14. Addition of toy will add variety to existing play setting
    •All developmental areas (physical, cognitive, emotional, social) are supported by toys present

15. Similar play value cannot be achieved by teacher- or parent-made toy
    •Choice is responsible since other possibilities have been considered

These criteria can help child care providers and parents choose appropriate toys. Choosing toys from reputable companies (such as those having a 1-800 customer service number printed on all items) and from reputable distributors (such as companies which offer excellent customer service) can help tremendously in choosing toys. Additionally, using sound play philosophy when choosing toys can enable adults to create appropriate learning environments for children.

Resources

Abrams, B. S. (1990). *Toys for early childhood development*. Atlanta, Ga.: The Center for Applied Research in Education.

Boehm, H. (1986). *The right toys*. New York: Bantam Books.

American Society for Testing and Materials. (1991). *Standard consumer safety specification on toy safety*. Chicago: Author.

LINDA G. MILLER, ED.D., is director of education for KinderCare Learning Centers, Inc., the largest proprietary child care corporation in the United States. She is responsible for choosing toys for KinderCare centers. Her doctorate in educational leadership is from Auburn University.

Chapter 16
Creating Urban Designs

JOANNE K. GUILFOIL

During the summer of 1990, Stanford University hosted the Playful City Conference on the assumption that the physical environment can support or hinder human development. Another assumption was that a city designed to support and nurture the development of our youth will support and nurture us all. The Playful City was a national response to the conditions and trends that have created unfriendly and unhealthy places for children, youth and families. The purpose of the conference was to include youth in the development of visions of urban environments where people feel welcome and at home, are comforted and protected, and can explore and discover life.[1] Throughout the conference and at the end, the youth asked for help with speaking, drawing imagining, working together and leadership skills. Children can practice and refine the same skills in school and other learning environments. Educating youth to participate in urban design can lead to more playful experiences and responsible roles in childhood and in adult life (Guilfoil, 1992a). This paper suggests some of the ways in which we can give children and youth such opportunities.

Play and Art
For children, play is both a source and outlet for their creative self-expression. In their play, we can discover the beginnings of a special kind of art that truly comes from the imagination of children (Szekely, 1991).

The theory of a relationship between play and art is based on six premises:

1. All children are artists, born with a natural ability to observe, formulate art ideas, and execute works of art on their own. For young children, play and art are inseparable. The longer this relationship lasts, the better individual creativity can be pursued.
2. When we offer children a playful environment, their excitement about their own ideas, sensations, and feelings will stimulate them to make art.
3. Children's art experiences should deal with the qualities of real materials within their environment, rather than techniques for creating illusions of real things.
4. Great art depends on movements emanating from both mind and body. Freedom of movement is essential in the art classroom because it generates the independent attitudes so necessary for the artist.
5. Children's performances in play are vital to the performance of making art. They provide the inspiration for the child artist to explore new movements, media and subjects for expression.
6. Art teaching is the celebration of the freedom to search for the artistic spirit in every person. The art teacher is the catalyst whose primary function is to create conditions within which children are inspired with their own ideas for making art (Szekely, 1991).

Playful and experimental environments created with words, actions and settings support and involve children, allowing their creative acts to surface. In classrooms, these "plays" involve an attitude of looking ahead and playing to discover art. Early "play" becomes a search, an engagement in a poetic act, and an illustration of how art is an accessible part of children's lives (Szekely, 1991, p. iii).

The Playful City Vision
During the 1990 conference, the youth provided constant reminders which at times were

loud and other times were deeply introspective comments, but were always accompanied by rich, symbolic, visual displays. Partly because of these influences, the overriding conclusion of adults in all of the conference work groups was the necessary involvement of youth in the design, maintenance, and evaluation of urban spaces.

By the end of the conference, the youth banded together and said "teach us" how to participate effectively so that our vision is clearly represented. Only then can planners "use our ideas in a more democratic process. It is our city, too," they said (Guilfoil, 1992a).

For those of us who worked with and for the youth, our charge is clear: We need to teach them visual thinking and group processes, some of which must center on the built environment. Art teachers already provide some visual thinking activities in their art classes. However, the youth said it was not enough and that the studio art courses rarely addressed environmental or urban planning themes.

Art education has a crucial role in the development of a playful city that effectively involves youth in urban design decisions. Art teachers can help keep the "play" in a playful city for us all through more curriculum development, instruction, teacher training, and research. Curriculum and instruction in built environment education should focus on visual thinking, architectural criticism, urban planning issues, children's play, play leadership training and cooperative learning. This public education should take place in school buildings and school yards where programs and settings are in part designed, maintained, and evaluated by the students (Guilfoil, 1992a). That is the work of the future as suggested by the youth during that conference in 1990. A few educators have been working with these ideas for years. The following are examples of their ideas, which combine playful strategies and art activities to help children and youth respond to their urban environment effectively and responsibly.

Sidewalks as Art Education

Neperud (1991) realized that hands-on projects can help young people develop environmental responsibility and greater awareness of the assumptions that affect our human-environment relationships. These ideas are useful to educators who are striving to include the built environment as subject and context for art education.

One such project is the design and construction of a brick sidewalk on school grounds.[2] Children of all ages can participate in the design and construction with the assistance of professionals and members of the community. During the project, children solve real design problems with all of the artistic, mathematical, political, and manual skills they can muster, and with on-the-spot advice from adults. The social, personal, and environmental experiences which the children have during the project are irreplaceable. The end products are reminders of their cooperative efforts for years to come.

With these projects in environmental design, the goal is to educate children toward an awareness and commitment necessary to engage environmental issues and to provide an effective vehicle for creative self-expression. Students need study and practice in the social and cultural contexts of art and the built environment and it must begin when they are young. The brick sidewalk is one of many projects which engages young people, serves an immediate functional need, answers an artistic/aesthetic problem, and documents an attitude about their place in the environment (Guilfoil, 1992b).

Box City

Moving beyond the confines of the school yard, another type of project is Box City, an interdisciplinary experience in city planning. Box City was initiated in 1969 by local architects and educators in Kansas City, Kansas to help educators develop an understanding of the built environment and its implications for students. Later developed as a unit of study about the city, it has been used in schools from elementary to college level, in museum education, and in architectural education classes for teachers (Graves, 1990).

In the Box City project, students are given boxes to alter and decorate to represent a particular type of building: industrial, residential, commercial, or public. Box sizes vary according to types of buildings. Boxes can be purchased or children can bring boxes from home.[3] Since a variety of buildings are needed for model town or city, it is helpful to organize a sign-up sheet or assign children to different types of buildings. The boxes are then decorated with paper, paint, or rubber stamps to encourage their knowledge of architectural details and styles (Graves, 1990).

Box City can be engaged in as an individual art class activity. However, it is more effective if used in a unit of study on the built environment involving a team of social studies and art teachers and a cooperative learning effort by the students. Students can learn about urban planning and relevant social, cultural, political, and economic issues and the influence of those issues on the creation of their box-buildings.

As a culminating group activity, it is important to create a model of the city using the box-buildings. A large street grid is designed and the buildings are placed along the streets to approximate a city or town. As a group, children discuss the location of each building. To help them understand the implications of zoning and planned development in city growth, teachers can appoint some children "city planners," whose job it is to approve or deny placement of buildings. The teacher faciliates the discussion until all buildings are placed. Students then compare and contrast the constructed city or town to their own, perhaps with a visit from an architect or city planner (Graves, 1990).

Box City incorporates concepts from history, geography, art, politics, city planning, and economics. Box City supports development of skills in cooperation, writing, art, mathematics, and spatial relationships, as well as an understanding of the present problems and future needs of cities. Box City offers opportunities for students of all ages and learning styles to participate successfully in group activities which refine skills needed to be a responsible and effective adult. Box City also involves imagination and, of course, play. Classroom teachers and art teachers now have a handy resource that explains the delicate balance between children's play and children's art and the environments in which they take place.

The Architectural Finds Play

In an extended classroom activity or "play"

called "Architectural Finds" (Szekley, 1991, p. 117), children begin by surveying the room for mock building lots, preferably ones with interesting ledges or views such as windows, shelves, corners, or chalk boards. "Building permits" are issued and the children discuss advantages and disadvantages of each site, assuming the roles of property owners or town councilors proposing or considering new construction.

Children then consider mock building materials such as brick, stone, blocks, hair curlers, PVC pipes, combs, and other novelties. They are challenged by the media and the freedom to select and test the materials while building their dream structures: homes, forts, monuments, towns, and cities. Some structures span chairs; others lean over a table edge; some structures are joined and rise to climb a wall. Each project requires many site plans, various phases of construction, some interior views, real estate ads and realtor walk-throughs, all created with art papers, stickers, tapes, labels and rubber stamps to simulate architectural elements on paper. Students observe their constructed city blocks, light them and study them from different distances, heights and angles.

Architechural Finds combines features of Box City and City Building Education Program (Nelson, 1984).[4] However, Szekely's focus here and in other activities is on children's play and art. His approach to urban design education is much more child-centered and play-oriented and is definitely child-directed and produced.

Szekely says future art teaching must be creative to foster creativity. We must set aside what we know as art to allow children to imagine beyond it, for even the most complex art problems become playful challenges,when posed as creative experiences. Rather than obstacles to be surmounted, art lessons can become hopeful experiences, providing abudant opportunities for independent investigation and discovery. We must also remember that our classrooms are filled with children, not art students. Szekely (1991) closes with a few suggestions for reaching these playful goals for all of us:

1. Make room for children's interests. Move from sandbox play to earth work design and

creation, from water play to watercolor experimentation, from block play to architectural design and from dollhouse play to the interior design of community and personal use spaces.

2. License children to play. Demonstrate playfulness regularly and welcome similar gestures from others.
3. Create opportunities for play. Invite children to enter a haunted house or castle, land on a treasure island or visit a junkyard. Rotate physical settings (new places, surfaces, spaces) to elicit new play starts.
4. Encourage discoveries. Pose art lessons as questions that challenge children to investigate and discover.
5. Foster independence with praise and by summarizing independent choices.
6. Add drama. Arrive with unexpected items.
7. Capitalize on the outdoors. Encourage large-scale designs with brick, corrugated drain pipes and floor tile.
8. Use creative timing to sustain student interest. Pace activities; time performances.

At best, students should associate art class with seeking art and ideas rather than receiving them. After all, the goal of art learning is making art without the teacher" (Szekely, 1991, p. 132).[5]

Summary

The purpose of this paper has been to address concerns raised by the youth who participated in the Playful City Conference and to suggest playful strategies in art and urban design education. The students said they wanted help with imaging, speaking, writing, visualizing, working together and leadership to better present their perspective, because they were not getting to practice these skills in school.

Art education can provide these needed experiences by involving youth in real and simulated urban design decisions and activities as part of art classes. These activities can be brief and simple or prolonged and complex.

All of the projects are celebrations of the children's imaginations, not recreations of adult-designed environments.

These projects suggested a wide range of activities involving children's play, art and built environment education. As we select and refine ideas for working with children and youth, we must remember the ultimate goal of environmental learning and all learning is their continued learning without the teacher. They are already doing it when they play.

References

Graves, G. (1990). *Box city*. Prairie Village, KS: Center for Understanding the Built Environment.

Guilfoil, J. K. (1992a). The playful city: A vision of the city through the eyes of young people. *Journal of Social Theory in Art Education* (in print).

Guilfoil, J. K. (1992b). Art and built environment education: Sidewalks as art education. Art Education, 45, (5), 17-24.

Nelson, D. (1984). *Transformations: Process and theory, a curriculum guide to creative development*. Santa Monica, CA: Center for City Building Educational Programs.

Neperud, R. W. (1991, March). A propositional view of environmental experiencing. Paper presented at a meeting of the National Art Education Association, Atlanta, GA.

Szekely, G. (1991). *From play to art*. Portsmouth, NH: Heinemann Educational Books, Inc.

Notes

1. The Playful City Project was initiated by PLAE, Inc. (Playing and Learning in Adaptable Environments) and funded in part by the National Endowment for the Arts. Playful City is a national effort to create design guidelines for the development of urban communities that support the needs of children. For more information write: PLAE, Inc.; 1802 Fifth Street, Berkeley, CA 94710; USA.
2. Over the last 20 years I have had the opportunity to supervise three brick sidewalk projects on three different school sites. For futher explanation of these projects see Guilfoil, J.K. (1992), Art and built environment education, *Art Education*, 45(5), 17-24.
3. A set of 40 boxes of various sizes and designs is available from C.U.B.E. (Center for Understanding the Built Environment), 5328 W. 67th Street, Prairie Village, KS 66208. The Classroom Pack also includes instructions, a

large grid, and bibliography. A Festival Pack of 1,000 boxes also is available. For more information write to Ginny Graves at the above address or call (913) 262-0691.

4. Another approach to city building as education is Doreen Nelson's (1984) City Building Education Program. Nelson provides a bold philosophy and curriculum for elementary teachers which utilizes the built environment of the city. Her hands-on approach connects learning with future experience and helps students develop creative thinking skills. Students begin by constructing a land site, then plan and build a boom town. No boxes or architectural styles are provided here. Rather, the idea is that they see the ways in which city life is altered, adapted and improved as changes which in turn transform the quality of life. Children are immediately and intimately engaged with the social, political and economic issues and concerns of a built environment.

5. George Szekely's *From Play to Art* reminds us to pay attention to children's play-oriented creativity, which is not only usually ignored, but usually considered trivial. For example, bathtub play prolongs bath time, play usually means "making a mess," and play at the dinner table is always rude or impolite. Rather, Szekely proposes a framework and major play ideas, including play environments, materials, movement, basic plays and artistic adaptations and examples from art classes. He closes with teaching tips and ideas for play designs in school art classes.

JOANNE K. GUILFOIL, PH.D., is associate professor of elementary art education at Eastern Kentucky University.

Chapter 17
Movement Structures: A Cooperative Play Activity

RHONDA CLEMENTS

Responding to our nation's changing demographics, the National Education Association has urged states to mandate early childhood programs in public schools by the year 2000. Recent newsletters for teachers and administrators report that more than 30 states now have children four years of age in their public schools, and some of these schools may enroll three-year-old children. This change stems from an increase in the number of single parents and of parents working outside the home (Hanson, 1992; Day, 1988).

The enrollment of three- and four-year-old children in public schools poses critical concerns for special subject teachers whose professional preparation has not included the competencies common to the early childhood discipline. This lack of knowlege is especially true in the area of physical education, due to a seemingly natural division made in the early 1920s in which theories of play development separated spontaneous play from organized games (Butler, Gotts, & Quisenberg, 1978). Play was considered to be instinctive, while the primary purpose of games was to transmit values of the culture. Subsequently, developmental play theory has not been an intricate component of the physical educator's training.

It was not until the late 1950s that experts in physical education recognized a need for content to replace the traditional sports and games program in the elementary school curriculum. An interaction with physical education specialists from England resulted in the adoption of movement education. Movement education, which is credited to the theories of Rudolph Laban, encouraged teachers: (a) to acknowledge "movement" as the primary emphasis for kindergarten through second-grade children,

(b) to implement the concepts in a series of units or themes, and (c) to use a problem-solving methodology to teach basic traveling and non-traveling motor skills in a noncompetitive atmosphere. This foundation changed the aim of the elementary child's lesson from only learning sport and game skills to that of acquiring a movement vocabulary, increasing one's awareness of the body's capabilities, and determining the purpose of movement.

Activity selection within Laban's framework encourages professionals to conceptualize movement experiences according to the following four foundation questions: What is the body capable of doing? (e.g., body awareness and body management activities); How can the body move? (e.g., applying differing degrees of force and speed while linking movements together smoothly); Where can the body move? (e.g., spatial awareness activities), and, With whom or with what can the body move? (e.g., relationships that exist with objects or people). These foundation questions have served as guidelines for selecting movement education activities for five- to eight-year-old children (Clements, 1988).

Very little research, however, has been given to selecting or creating physical activities that are developmentally appropriate for three- or four-year-old children. In fact, very few movement education activities have been included in textbooks related to early childhood education and its value has even been questioned. Hendrick (1990), for example, cautions teachers about using this approach. The author, like several others, favors using creative dance activities in contrast to those of movement education. A need exists for early childhood educators, childhood development specialists, and physical educators to exchange research and information related to play theories and movement theories in order to select or create the most developmentally appropriate physical activities for preschool children.

Characteristics of Physical Development

Since the extent to which the child participates depends largely on his or her sensory motor capabilities, it is logical to initiate the investigation process by identifying several characteristics that have a great importance for educators responsible for planning gross motor play situations. For instance, there is evidence in motor learning and perceptual motor research that preschool children are generally farsighted because of the foreshortening of the eyeball which does not reach its most spheroidal form until the age of six or seven years (Smith, 1970; Arnheim & Sinclair, 1979; Papalia & Olds, 1986; Kavner, 1985). Practitioners should incorporate the use of visual objects that are large enough to be clearly seen. This is especially important when planning experiences that challenge the child to concentrate on a target. The goal is most appropriate when the target is large and distinctly marked. In addition, the velocity of objects (e.g., yarnballs) tossed or propelled toward the child should be slow to allow for gradual focal convergence (Smith, 1970; Kavner, 1985).

Teachers of movement education also realize that it is advantageous to use equipment of various colors and intensities while teaching ball skills in kindergarten and first and second grade. Studies indicate that in this age group, both genders prefer blue, followed by red and orange (Smith, 1970). This color factor has less influence on preschool children, according to research on visual discrimination, since there is a greater tendency for these children to rely on the shape or form of an object for identification and classification than on the color (Smith, 1970; Papalia & Olds, 1986; Gallahue, 1985). This evidence reinforces the value of providing clay, sand, and mud which can be modeled into different forms (Butler, Gotts, & Quisenberg, 1978). In a gymnasium, also, practitioners should implement activities that reinforce shape, figure, and structure.

There is evidence that the young child's depth perception and size constancy are largely a function of the use of visual cues (Arnheim & Sinclair, 1979; Gallahue, 1985). It is therefore imperative that the young child's active play surroundings provide many varied visual cues. One technique includes placing arrows on the floor to guide the child's movement around obstacles. When using targets, practitioners should consider directing the child's point of focus by touching the designated target instead of standing beside the child throughout the propelling action. The circumference of the equipment used to teach grasping, rolling, tossing, and catching skills should also vary in size to expand the child's ability to adjust to different fielding situations (Nichols, 1991; Gallahue, 1985).

The process by which the young child's auditory rhythmical skills mature is extremely complex. In the simplest terms, the child's temporal perception involves the identification of a series of sounds interspersed by moments of silence in repeated patterns. In studies reflecting temporal perception, it was found that children make temporal discrimination through the auditory mode (Garvey, 1977; Smith, 1970). Hence, basic auditory rhythmic experiences in which the children are challenged to clap their hands or use a shaking device to match the practitioner's rate should be included. This type of "copy me" activity can be made more challenging by varying the speed in which the child must respond or by varying the volume (Butler, Gotts, & Quisenberry, 1978; Gallahue, 1985).

Numerous research studies have been performed on young children's tactile perception. The majority of this research focuses on the toddler's ability to gain information from the surfaces of the body by means of active contact such as grasping, reaching and possessing, and by passive contact like touching and feeling. Practitioners of physical activity should recognize that young children have greater tactile perception in their upper body (Arnheim & Sinclair, 1979; Butler, Gotts, & Quisenberg, 1978). In other words, the receptors of the head, mouth, fingers and palms are more sensitive to tactile sensations than are the lower extremities. Thus, tasks involving the upper body, such as the log roll, the forward roll, and the side roll should be implemented in addition to activities involving the trunk.

Additional implications include varying the

surfaces in which physical activity occurs. Outdoor play areas should include unobstructed flat surfaces, bumps, hills, and a variety of surfaces on which to play (e.g., asphalt, grass, wood chips) (Clements, 1992; Frost, 1992). Likewise, specialists should purchase equipment of varying textures (e.g., rubber playground balls, plastic beach balls, foam balls, and yarn balls) for more stimulating tactile experiences.

The young child's kinesthetic sense, which gives an individual feedback regarding the positioning of body segments, is in a critical stage of development (Smith, 1970). As a result, there are three distinct implications for the preschool activity specialist. First, physical activity programs for three- and four-year-old children should offer an extensive list of body part identification activities. Secondly, activities should challenge children to use specific body parts to perform tasks. Finally, teachers should use verbal cues that assist the young child in attending to proprioceptive feedback (e.g., "Look to see where you have placed your hands."). These three teaching techniques are used throughout the country in privately-owned gymnastic facilities for toddlers.

In addition to the preceding sensory modalities, balance mechanisms enable the three- or four-year-old to control his body orientation in space. Accordingly, these vestibular organs are stimulated by changes in direction or movement (Smith, 1970). This characteristic supports the need for a variety of spatial orientation activities involving dynamic as well as static balance.

Characteristics of Social Development

It is of equal importance to recognize several characteristics of the young child's social development. The following characteristics are generally agreed upon by specialists in the areas of psychology, sociology, and childhood learning theories, and they can be used by practitioners while planning developmentally appropriate affective objectives. To begin, the three-year-old child is at a highly imaginative stage of development. This vivid imagination is demonstrated when the child shrieks at loud noises, views shadows as threatening beings, and envisions monsters hiding in closets (Hughes, 1991). In the classroom setting, the child enjoys imitating the activities common to adults, such as those exhibited by family members (e.g., carpentry work and cooking). They also mimic the roles performed by community workers, and the behaviors common to animals, as well as the actions or sounds associated with certain objects.

In most cases, the child shares these imaginary play fantasies with one or more classmates and develops a form of appreciation for peer contribution. This type of peer interaction reflects the child's early attempts to form friendships. Friendships are formed when two or more children find similarities in their play interests (Cooper and Edward, 1985). These feelings are expressed in the phrase "my playmate" or in the child's identification of "the people I like." The implication for this factor rests on the teacher's ability to implement activites that reinforce how much fun it is to play with other children. The notion of incorporating rules to govern these play activities is viewed as necessary, for these restrictions are used for the good of everyone (Damon, 1979; Howes, 1992; Garvey, 1977).

When given the opportunity, the three-year-old child is capable of identifying, organizing, categorizing, and manipulating play objects to carry out imaginary plots. Large scale accessories or props for play experiences include child-size tableware, baking play sets, play food sets, kitchen sets, and dress-up outfits. Blocks can also be used to promote imaginative play episodes. Unlike the two-year-old's interest in stacking blocks, the three-year-old child uses blocks to build structures that coincide with the home and school environment (e.g., tunnels, streets, and buildings). These block sets offer a variety of shapes including arches, triangles, cylinders, animal figures, road signs, and greenery (Segal & Adcock, 1981). These specialized shapes and features enable children to add height and width dimensions to their structures (Butler, Gotts, & Quisenberry, 1978). Thereafter, the child experiences an increased sense of accomplishment when the completed structures are displayed to classmates and onlookers (Hughes, 1991).

In general, the three-year-old's social development falls within Parten's (1932) associative play pattern. The child still plays alongside classmates while performing separate activities, yet has an increased desire to share materials, to wait for his turn, and to communicate personal needs (Hughs, 1991; Papalia & Olds, 1986).

Four-year-old children display greater self-confidence through increased vocabulary and ability to follow sequences of directions (e.g., listening and successfully repeating words of a song). Interlocking building blocks, musical instruments, sequence puzzles, pegboard activities, games involving matching, and board games present enjoyable challenges for this age. They also exhibit a greater fascination with adult roles and have a greater awareness of gender differences (Hughes, 1991; Papalia & Olds, 1986). The desire for adult attention helps explain the child's somewhat unruly requests such as "Look at me!"

One developmentally appropriate means of fulfilling the child's need for attention and positive reinforcement is by providing conditions that facilitate small-group interaction. Parten classified the four-year-old's play as cooperative. Cooperative play occurs when the child engages in group activities having a common goal or theme (Singer and Singer, 1990; Papalia & Olds, 1986; Hughes, 1991; Frost, 1992; Kruger & Kruger, 1989; Hendrick, 1990). This mutual goal is accomplished when two or more children perform designated tasks and integrate their actions for a common purpose. In the classroom, for example, cooperative play might consist of four-year-olds sharing connecting blocks and jointly building a bridge for miniature cars. This behavior can be achieved in the gymnasium when two or more children use their bodies to form a bridge and permit others to move underneath. The latter example demonstrates the four-year-olds' strong urge for movement and interest in social interaction.

An Interdisciplinary Approach

As indicated earlier, very little research has been done to determine or suggest physical education activities that are developmentally appropriate for three- and four-year-old children. At Hofstra University, a preschool physical education network, The Little Steps Network, was developed in 1989 to facilitate communication between eight Long Island (New

York) preschool and nursery schools that were desiring cooperative play activities. Under the direction of the faculty in Hofstra's Graduate Physical Education Program, the network's primary functions have been to: (a) establish curriculum development goals conducive to the parties involved, (b) provide field sites for graduate physical education students to implement and assess the effectiveness of selected cooperative movement activities, and (c) provide a forum in which the school's early childhood teachers discuss class observations and increase their understanding of movement concepts. The overall goal of this interdisciplinary network has been to exchange information related to childhood social development and movement theories in hopes of selecting or creating developmentally appropriate physical education activity content for three- and four-year-old children.

To do so, the network relied on the preceding physical and social characteristics to serve as a general basis of understanding among the parties involved. Network meetings were used to discuss selected activities that fell within the curriculum areas of movement experiences, ball skills, rhythmic skills, and fitness-related activities. In the third year of the investigation, attempts were made to create a specialized activity to specifically support the social and physical capabilities of this age group. The newly-developed content was given the name "Movement Structures."

Movement Structures

There is continuing controversy in early childhood education concerning the extent to which physical experiences should be provided for three- and four-year-old children and how the activities should be organized. The value and use of Movement Structures will most likely add to this debate. Nonetheless, few educators oppose new attempts to provide additional insight into the young child's social and physical capabilities. For this reason, the primary function and strategies for implementing Movement Structures will be addressed.

To begin, Movement Structures were created for children in the Little Steps Network to serve as a basis for more advanced learning experiences. The term is defined as "the three- to four-year-old child's specific use of individual body parts to produce developmentally appropriate and identifiable shapes, objects, and traveling actions." The inclusion of the term "developmentally appropriate" indicates that the activity is designed for the developmental status, previous movement experiences, fitness and skill, body size, and age (Council on Physical Education for Children, 1992). In total, 112 movement structures were developed and field-tested. Eighty structures were selected for their appropriateness and appeal.

The teacher's role: Like all purposeful learning experiences, using Movement Structures requires some teacher preparation. At a quick glance, most preschool settings provide all of the necessary materials, teacher resources, and equipment for participation in this activity. The key element, however, is the teacher's competency or willingness to select and add movement activities that are relevant to the children's cognitive understanding and interest. These selected structures provide the stimulus for distinctive movement and interaction.

The five-step teaching process begins with a brief introduction in which the teacher conveys factual information related to the selected movement structure (i.e., an object, shape, or thing). This step is facilitated by the use of photographs, miniature figurines, or illustrations of the selected structure to increase the child's motivation and understanding. The children typically are sitting or standing in a group. Following this brief introduction, in Step Two the teacher challenges the children to use particular body parts to imitate the structure's form or physical characteristics. In Step Three, the child is challenged to move while displaying the imitated structure. In Step Four, this imitated structure is applied to either a game, a gymnastic, a dance, or a fitness-related activity. The Fifth and final step includes the teacher's assessment of the child's interaction and performance. The following example demonstrates this process.

The Penguin: In Step One, the practitioner uses a picture book to spark the children's interest

and conveys information about the penguin. The information should reflect characteristics related to the animal's body (e.g., penguins have slender heads, long pointed beaks and short legs and waddle when they walk. Adult Penguins are three feet tall. The wings stay at the side of the body and act as oars and fins to push them through the water.) After the information is delivered, the practitioner asks the children to compare the penguin's body to their own (e.g., "The penguin has a long pointed beak. What body part do we have that is like the penguin's beak?" Or, "The penguin's wings are at the sides of the body. What two body parts do we have at the sides of our bodies?"). This introductory step usually takes from three to five minutes, depending on the availability and relevance of the information.

In Step Two, the children are challenged to use their bodies to waddle like the penguin (e.g., "Let's pretend that you are a community of penguins waddling across the ice. Can you stand very tall like the King Penguins who live in the Antarctic, where it is very cold?" "Who can keep their legs very stiff and take a tiny step forward with one leg and then take a step foward with the other?" "This is how the penguin waddles along the ice, shifting one side of the body at a time." "Can you keep your arms at the sides of your body while you waddle?")

In Step Three, the children are encouraged to move around the room or playground, waddling and imitating the movement of the penguin.

In Step Four, the teacher incorporates the Movement Structure into either a game or fitness, dance, or gymnastic activity. The Giant Iceberg Game challenges individuals to waddle in a specific playing space (i.e., an imaginary iceberg) without touching their classmates' bodies. At some point, the teacher signals for the penguins to "freeze" or stop moving. The playing space is made smaller by using some form of cones or markers. This change in available playing space symbolizes a melting iceberg. The process is repeated until the iceberg becomes too small for the penguins. At this point, the children are encouraged to "jump off the iceberg" into imaginary water. They use their arms as fins to swim to the safety of another iceberg (i.e., a different designated playing space).

The Penguin Parade gymnastic activity encourages the individual to follow a partner's selected pathway while maintaining the waddling movement throughout the playing area. At some point, the teacher asks the children to exchange leader/follower roles. The activity is completed by having the entire class form a line with their bodies and follow the teacher in a parade of penguins.

The fitness activity, The Penguin's Skating Rink, requires active movement as the children maintain the characteristics of the Movement Structure and follow arrows through a teacher-designated obstacle course. This obstacle course includes "pretend" skating rinks outlined by chalk, tape, or cones. The children may break away from the Movement Structure to explore a variety of skating movements inside each designated rink but must revert to the movement structure as they continue onward through the course. The teacher varies the number of rinks according to available space and physical limitations.

The Melting Iceberg Song (words by Joyce Zucker) incorporates the Movement Structure into a rhythmical learning experience by having the children sing and react to the following words:

Penguins standing on the ice
They think the ice is nice
But the sunshine in the day
Starts to melt the ice away

(Children demonstrate the penguin's characteristics (i.e., the Movement Structure, as they move throughout a large circular area.)

(Chorus)
And they have to move a little closer
And they have to move a little closer
And they have to move a little closer
And they have to move a little closer

(Children take short, quick steps as they move one side of the body and then the other side to waddle without touching classmates' bodies.)

Then, the ice becomes much too small,

Much too small to hold them all
So they slide and slide and leap
They all splash into the deep

(Children continue to waddle and perform the slide, leap, and splashing motion.)

And they swim away a little faster
And they swim away a little faster
And they swim away a little faster
And they swim away a little faster

(Children use their arms like fins and perform a swimming motion away from the circle.)

Until they all will meet once more
On a cold and icy shore
And they'll stand there on the ice
For they think the ice is nice

(Children return to the circle and repeat the penguin's characteristics and movement.)

Repeat chorus.

In the Fifth Step of this movement structure, the children discuss their participation. They are reminded that their bodies are very special and can move in a variety of ways (e.g., "What body parts did you use to move like the penguin?"). The teacher also uses this time to review information about penguins or to draw from the children's personal experiences and memories (e.g., trips to the zoo, television programs about penguins).

The discussion helps the teacher determine how the children perceive their bodies' capabilities and how these capabilities contribute to group success. Hence, Movement Structures provide one means in which preschool children can make the transition from cooperative play to organized activities and games with rules.

References

Arnheim, D. D. & Sinclair, W. A. (1979). *The clumsy child: A program of motor therapy* (2nd ed.). St. Louis: C. V. Mosby Co.

Butler, A. L. Gotts, E. E., & Quisenberry, N. L. (1978). *Play as development*. Columbus, Ohio: Merrill.

Clements, R. (1988). A multi-case study of the implementation of movement education in selected schools. Unpublished doctoral dissertation, Teachers College, Columbia University.

Clements, R. (1992). Equipment of an outdoor playground for children: Birth to age eight. In Fromberg, D. P. & Williams, L. R. (Eds.), *Encyclopedia of early childhood education*. New York: Garland Press.

Cooper, C. & Edward, D. (1985). Playfriends and workfriends: Developmental patterns in the meaning and function of children's friendships. In Frost, J. L. & Sunderlin, S. (Eds.), *When children play: Proceedings of the international conference on play and play environments*. Wheaton, Md.: Association for Childhood Education International.

Council on Physical Education for Children. (1992). *Developmentally approprite physical education practices for children*. Reston, Va.: National Association for Sport and Physical Education.

Damon, W. (1979). *The social world of the child* (2nd ed.). San Francisco: Jossey-Bass Publishers.

Day, B. D. (1988). What's happening in early childhood programs across the United States. In Warger, C. (Ed.), *A resource guide to public school early childhood programs*. Alexandria, Va.: Curriculum Development Publications.

Frost, J. L. (1992). *Play and playscapes*. Albany, N.Y.: Delmar Publishers, Inc.

Gallahue, D. L. (1985). *Developmental movement experiences for children* (2nd ed.). New York: Macmillan.

Garvey, C. (1977). *Play*. Cambridge, Mass.: Harvard University Press.

Hanson, M. R. (1992). Physical educators must prepare for preschoolers in the public schools. *Teaching Elementary Physical Education*, 3(1), 1-7.

Hendrick, J. (1990). *Total learning: Developmental curriculum for the young child* (3rd ed.). Columbus, Ohio: Merrill.

Howes, C. Unger, O., & Matheson, C. C. (1992). *The collaborative construction of pretend: Social pretend play functions*. Albany, N.Y.: State University of New York Press.

Hughes, F. P. (1991). *Children, play, and development*. Boston: Allyn and Bacon.

Kavner, R. S. (1985). *Your child's vision: A parent's guide to seeing, growing, and developing*. New York: Simon and Schuster.

Kruger, H. & Kruger, J. (1989). The preschool teacher's guide to movement education. Baltimore, Md.: Gerstung Publications.

Nichols, B. (1991). *Moving and learning: The elementary school physical education experience* (2nd ed.). St. Louis, Mo.: Times Mirror/ Mosby.

Paplia, D. E. & Olds, S. W. (1986). *Human development* (3rd ed.). New York: McGraw-Hill.

Parten, M. (1932). Social participation among preschool children. *Journal of Abnormal and Social Psychology*, 27, 243-369.

Segal, M. & Adcock, D. (1981). *Just pretending: Ways to help children grow through imaginative play*. Englewood Cliffs, N.J.: Prentice-Hall.

Singer, D. & Singer, J. L. (1990). *The house of make believe: Children's play and developing imagination*. Cambridge, Mass.: Harvard University Press.

Smith, H. M. (1970). Implications for movement education experiences drawn from perceptual-motor research. *Journal of Health, Physical Education, Recreation and Dance*, 41(4), 30-33.

RHONDA CLEMENTS is coordinator of graduate physical education at Hofstra University in Hempstead, New York. She is the developer and coordinator of the Little Steps Preschool Physical Education Network.

Part VI
Children's Play: Beyond General Practice

General practice in medicine encompasses routine examinations and the general knowledge of health. What is considered "general practice" in the professional field of play? The four papers in this section link theory to practice by reviewing the classic theories of play and applying them to movement activities, to opening new areas of investigation beyond Piagetian stages, to finding ways to assess cognitive development outdoors, and to analyzing play behaviors as influenced by outdoor equipment choices.

Keller and **Weiller** provide a historical overview and current definitions of the importance of play from Shiller and Spencer (1870's) to Bammel and Bammel (1982). From theory, Keller and Weiller propose specific play experiences and activity challenges for children. Their work is influenced by the overriding philosophy of making experiences appropriate and meaningful for children.

Theories, by definition, are "educated guesses" based on the best empirical knowledge at any given time. Thus, the theories currently studied and examined by scholars in the field of play need to be pushed to further the study of play. **Reifel** pushes our study of play further by examining what new scholars find missing in some of the most popular theories. In doing such, the reader will grow and be better able to plan play experiences for children.

Too often, outdoor play is viewed as recess or merely physical development. In such a view, the potential for assessing cognitive development in the outdoors is overlooked. **Fox** reports through a series of outdoor play anecdotes and analyses several specific examples of children's knowledge or mastery of academic skills.

The final paper in this grouping is a quantitative study of third-grade children's social and cognitive play behaviors and equipment choices on contrasting playgrounds. **Frost, Yang, Horney, Chin** and **Lin** continue the examination of playgrounds across America started by the National Survey of Elementary School Playground Equipment and the National Survey of American Preschool. They zero in with this study using observation ratings, time samplings and anecdotal notes. The study found that cognitive play behaviors differ substantially across play environments, while the overall social play behaviors were very similar.

Chapter 18
Creating Meaningful Play Experiences with Children:
Linking Play Theories to Practice

M. Jean Keller
Karen H. Weiller

Play is universal and vital to human development and existence. It offers positive contributions to all areas of development and is beneficial in all stages of life. Play can be described as a condition in which learning may flourish and the cognitive structures of the mind can be allowed to optimally function (Frost & Klein, 1979; Sponseller, 1974). Though the importance and value of play have long been understood, a resurgence of recognition of play's inportance occurred in the 1970s as society began to shift from a work to a leisure ethic. This rediscovery of the value of play prompted further investigation of the nature and function of this unique phenomenon (Frost & Klein, 1979). Creating meaningful play experiences is an important task for individuals involved with children as educators, recreation professionals, child care providers, and parents. However, determining what activities or experiences are appropriate for children can be quite challenging. This paper will address this significant issue by examining what play is and the important role it has for children, providing a reflective look at selective theories of play, and linking these theories with practical applications.

Definitions and Characteristics of Play

Play is the dominant expression and outlet for children and is an integral factor in their continuous quest for development (Bergen, 1988). Definitions of this critical process have been provided from diverse viewpoints, by a variety of theorists. Early theorists such as Schiller (1875), Spencer (1873), and Gulick (1920) suggested that play was superfluous actions taking place instinctively in the absence of real actions. Furthermore, these theorists submitted that play activity was an aimless expenditure of exuberant energy, performed for immediate gratification with little regard for ulterior benefits. Gulick put forth that play was an activity which was done simply because one wanted to do so.

More recently, Piaget (1962) and Garvey (1977) added to the growing variety of definitions of play. Piaget asserted that play served as both a mechanism for knowing about the world and for gaining an insight into children's levels of cognitive development. Garvey suggested that play was connected to aspects of creativity, problem solving, language acquisition, and development of social roles. Garvey further suggested that "play is most frequent in a period of dramatically expanding knowledge of self, the physical and social world, and systems of communication" (1977, p. 1).

Elements and criteria of what actually could be defined as play have encompassed many frames of thought. Spodek, Soracho, & Davis (1987) reported that these definitions have spanned a range from structural (typical movements) to functional (enjoyable activity). These authors emphasized the legitimacy of play.

In recent years, several researchers have sought to delineate criteria which would lead towards a clearer and better understanding of the phenomenon of play. Neumann (1971) identified three criteria to be used in judging how an activity was to be classified on the play/work continuum. These were:

*Control: Activities which lean towar*d being internally controlled were considered closer to play than those activities which were externally controlled. Neumann, however, pointed out that an individual could only totally control his own play when playing alone.

Reality: Activities which allow individuals to suspend reality and enter into a pretend or "as if" quality were considered to be associated with play.

Motivation: Although activities are seldom considered totally internally or externally motivated, Neumann (1977) considered activities which were internally motivated to be closer to the play end of the play-work continuum.

In further identifying criteria which might be used to address a definiton or description of play, the work of Rubin, Fein, & Vandenberg (1983), Smith and Vollstedt (1985), and Bergen (1988) added to the body of knowledge. Rubin, et. al. noted, as had others in the past, that play was internally based and free from externally-imposed rules. Both active engagement and focusing on the means rather than the ends were vital facets in defining play (Rubin, et al., 1983).

Smith and Vollstedt (1985) and Bergen (1988) sought to identify criteria to ensure proper classification of play behavior. Smith and Vollstedt proposed the use of three criteria to be used when judging play activity. When watching children at play, these authors noted that observers had reported play activities of children to be enjoyable, flexible, and make-believe. Using play as a medium for learning, Bergen adopted Webster's (1980) multiple definitions of the word *play*. Play was all encompassing and allowed children to gain mastery over their environment (Bergen, 1988). She further suggested that as children were often less able to effectively use language as a means of communication, play became the channel through which their feelings and thoughts were relayed. Bergen reported that children often become totally engrossed in their play activities, oftentimes using play as a means of self-expression in a risk-free environment.

Role of Play for Children

Although play is difficult to define and observe, it appears to serve a needed function. Adults and children alike play. Just as adults express themselves in a creative manner (Bergen, 1988), children explore their world through dramatic and creative play. Children learn, grow, and develop physically, mentally, socially, and emotionally through their play experiences. Play can enhance overall development by allowing children to master traumatic experiences, practice previously-learned skills, develop abstract thinking, and promote strength, endurance, and flexibility, in behavior and thinking (Ellis, 1973). Children communicate their thoughts and feelings through play and demonstrate their understanding of the thoughts and feelings of others and of the world around them. It is vital for all individuals involved in children's development to value play as a critical learning tool for gaining competencies necessary for future success in society (Bergen, 1988; Toffler, 1980).

Play Theories

The question, "Why do children play?" has spawned many theories that try to establish the basic nature and motive for play. The following play theories, classical, contemporary, and recent, can enhance understanding of how to create meaningful play experiences for children.

Classical Theories of Play

Historically, play theories have developed as a result of objective, scientific and subjective, nonscientific endeavors. Most early theories of play sought to explain play behavior in terms of nonscientific physiological bases. One of the most influential theories of play was that of surplus energy, which emerged in the late 1800's through the writing of Schiller (a poet) and Spencer (a philosopher). This theory suggested that play was caused by energy surplus to the needs of survival (Sessoms, 1986). Thus, play was essentially purposeless, although play outlets were necessary in order to vent the exuberant energy of children.

At the same time that this surplus energy theory was prominent, Karl Groos proposed the instinct-practice theory in 1898, suggesting that play, rather than being an aimless activity, was the means by which children practiced and perfected the skills they would need in adult life (Kraus, 1984). Using Darwin's theory of evolution as a foundation, Groos developed an extended theory involving physiological, psychological, aesthetic, and sociological elements to explain his view of play behaviors. By assigning a biological purpose to play, Groos influenced early educators and recreation professionals in accepting the need for play in schools and in parks (Sessoms, 1986).

BEYOND GENERAL PRACTICE

The early designers of play experiences for children interpreted these theories to mean that play should be a means of relieving excess energy (surplus energy) and for practicing or repeating gross motor skills (instinct-practice). As a result, open playing fields with swings and slides became a norm for playgrounds. In fact, consistent with early theories which emphasized excess energy and physical training, these early parks and playgrounds were called outdoor gymnasiums (Frost, 1988).

As time progressed, these early play theories fell into some disregard (Bruner, Jolly, & Sylva, 1976) as more contemporary theories based on a growing body of scienfic evidence

began to emerge. Contemporary play theories expanded the early theories" emphasis on exercise and motor activities to a comprehensive view of children's play behavior as developmental and educational experiences (Piaget, 1962; Sutton-Smith, 1970).

Contemporary Theories of Play

One of the leaders of this movement was Piaget (1962), who linked the developmental progression of play to stages of cognitive development. According to Piaget, play results from the imbalance of two cognitive processes, assimilation and accommodation. Assimilation occurs when an object or received information is

Classical Theories of Play			
Theory	Play is caused:	This explanation assumes:	It can be criticized because:
Surplus Energy	by the existence of energy surplus to the needs of survival.	1. Energy is stored. 2. Storage is limited. 3. Excess energy must be expended. 4. Expenditure is made through play.	1. Children play when fatigued or to the point of fatigue so a surplus is not necessary for play. 2. The process of evolution should have tailored the energy available to the energy required.
Instinct	by the inheritance of unlearned capacities to emit playful acts.	1. The determinants of our behavior are inherited in the same way that we inherit the genetic code that determines our make-up. 2. That some of those determinants cause play.	1. It ignores the obvious capacity of the person to learn new responses that we classify as play. 2. The facile naming of an instinct for each class of learned behavior is to do no more than to say "Because there is play, there must be a cause

Figure 1: Theories of Play [adapted from *Why People Play* (Ellis, 1973)].

A RIGHT TO PLAY **117**

adjusted to an individual's personal adjustment to the reality to personal needs. Accommodation is an individual's personal adjustment to the reality of an object or piece of information, by adjusting to the reality of the external world. Piaget contended that play indicated a preponderance of assimilation, in which real events are distorted to the level of a person's cognitive level. For example, a child assimilates when an empty box becomes a play car. Accommodation occurs when the child wants real wheels for the box car (Bammel & Bammel, 1982).

Piaget theorized that intellectual development proceeds through a hierachy of stages: *sensory-motor, preoperational, concrete operational,* and *formal operational* (see Figure 2).

Stage one of the cognitive development theory of play for children involves sensory-motor development. This most basic form of play involves touching, tasting, hearing, smell-

Contemporary Theories of Play			
Theory	Play is caused:	This explanation assumes:	It can be criticized because:
Developmental	by the growth of the child's intellect and is conditioned by it; play occurs when the child can impose on reality his own conceptions and constraints.	1. That play involves the intellect. 2. That as a result of play, the intellect increases in complexity. 3. That this process in the human can be separated into stages. 4. That children pass through these stages in order.	1. It does not account for play when and if the intellect ceases to develop.
Learning	by the normal processes that produce learning.	1. The child acts to increase the probability of pleasant events. 2. The child acts to decrease the probability of unpleasant events. 3. The environment is a complex of pleasant and unpleasant effects. 4. The environment selects and energizes the play behaviors of its tenants.	1. It does not account for behavior in situations where there are no apparent consequences. (However, this theory would maintain that there are no such settings.) 2. It does not account for the original contributions to behaviors made by an individual's genetic inheritance.

Figure 1, cont.: Theories of Play [adapted from *Why People Play* (Ellis, 1973)].

ing, and seeing. Concepts such as repetition, reproduction, and generalization are also aspects of this phase of cognitive development. For instance, once learned, activities such as catching a ball or sliding down an incline are repeated for the sensation the activity yields and the satisfaction of mastering it.

The preoperational stage of cognitive development is characterized by symbolic or make-believe play where one object can represent another. Thus, a swing may become an airplane and monkey bars may be used to traverse a stream filled with alligators. "Upon passage from stage to stage within the preoperation phase, the child gradually perceives more and more of reality. Play becomes modified as perceptions of reality are incorporated. The symbolic play objects come close to the real thing" (Bammel & Bammel, 1982, p. 50).

By the time a child reaches the third stage of

Recent or Modern Theories of Play			
Theory	Play is caused:	This explanation assumes:	It can be criticized on the grounds that:
Play as Arousal-seeking	by the need to generate intereactions with the environment or self that elevates arousal (level of interest or stimulation) towards the optimal for the child.	1. Stimuli vary in their capacity to arouse. 2. There is a need for optimal arousal. 3. Change in arousal towards optimal is pleasant. 4. The child learns the behaviors that result in that feeling and vice versa.	1. It is very general and handles equally well questions of work and play. In fact, it questions the validity of distinguishing work from play.
Competence /Effectance	by a need to produce effects in the environment. Such effects demonstrate competence and result in feelings of effectance.	1. Demonstration of competence leads to feelings of effectance. 2. Effectance is pleasant. 3. Effectance increases the probability of tests of competence.	1. For the child to constantly test where he can still competently produce an effect seems to require uncertainty as to the outcome. Uncertainty or information seem to be the very attributes of stimuli that are arousing. 2. Thus it can be argued that competence/effectance behavior is a kind of arousal-seeking.

Figure 1, cont.: Theories of Play [adapted from *Why People Play* (Ellis, 1973)].

Four Stages of Play Related to Development Theory		
Developmental Stage	Play Typology	Approximate Age
Sensory Motor	Practice	0-2
Preoperational	Symbolic	3-7
Concrete Operational	Games with Rules	8-11
Formal Operations	Transition to Adult Play	12 and older

Figure 2: Aadapted from *Leisure and Human Behavior* (Bammel & Bammel, 1982).

cognitive development, concrete operations, she replaces symbolic play with collective games which have formal rules. "Emergence of games with rules marks the decline of children's games and the transition to adult play" (Bammel & Bammel, 1982, p. 51).

The final phase or stage of cognitive development, concrete operations, involves play which follows prescribed rules of the game. Thus, the Little League of a seven-year-old child may still have elements of fantasy in which the child pretends to be a major league player, while an 11-year-old plays more competitively and the final winner is the important element.

Recent Theories of Play

There are two modern theories of play: play as *competence-motivation* and play as *arousal-seeking*. These theories have their origin in objective data. The recent view of play emphasizes the psychological importance of creative exploration, leading to stimulus-arousal and ultimately to creative enrichment and self-actualization. Leading to self-actualization are both the *stimulus-arousal* and the *competence-effectance* theories of play.

The arousal-seeking theory of play portrays play as a drive to seek stimuli of various kinds and to resolve or react to them in ways that provide excitement, satisfaction, or pleasure (Ellis, 1973). Three principles for play derived from the arousal-seeking model are:

1. Children play for the stimulation they receive.
2. This stimulation must contain elements of

uncertainty such as novelty, complexity, or dissonance.
3. Interactions producing stimulation must increase in complexity with accumulation of knowledge about or experience with play objects, activities, or areas (Ellis, 1973).

Applied to play experience, this theory implies that areas, activities, and materials are needed to provide for multiple levels of abilities so that children are challenged without unreasonable demands on their capabilities. Ideally, there would be enough challenge present to stimulate children to strive for the next level or goal. As children become familiar with certain play activities, variations such as size and complexity of materials, would provide the novelty needed to stimulate and sustain the play experience.

A closely-related play theory is competence-effectance. This theory is based on the idea that play is motivated by children's needs to test their environments, solve problems, and gain a sense of mastery and accomplishment. Beyond this, children seek to develop "competence" defined as the ability to interact effectively with the environment. This competence-based theory has some elements of the arousal-seeking theory in it; in fact, competence has been shown to be a facet of arousal-seeking stimuli (Csikszentimaihalyi, 1975). This theory supports the notion that play experiences should be selected according to children's sizes, abilities, and potentials so that competence can be achieved by the players.

In summary, play theories have evolved to a broader conceptual base over the past 90 years.

Recent theories have shifted the focus of play from being an outlet for physical conditioning and surplus energy for children to the idea that play is an important part of the long-term growth and development of the child's social, emotional, psychological, and cognitive domains. Having taken a brief look at several play theories, a logical question is, How have these theories been applied to the development and design of play experiences?

Applying the Theories

Educators, recreation leaders, child care providers, and parents are in influential and critical positions. These individuals, who come in contact with children on a daily basis, provide play experiences for children of a variety of ages. Applying a knowledge base to practical situations can enable adults to supply positive and growth-producing play experiences.

Providing children with activities which are appropriate to their developmental levels is quite critical (Nichols, 1990; Pangrazi & Dauer, 1992). Nichols and Pangrazi and Dauer advocate division of children into three developmental levels. The first level comprises early movement experiences. It is an important time for development of fundamental motor skills. As children learn and are introduced to basic locomotor (hopping, skipping, galloping) and manipulative (throwing, catching, kicking) skills, opportunities should be made available for continued practice of these skills. Repetition of activities not only yields satisfaction from enjoyment, but from improvement and mastery as well. Young children should be provided with opportunities to practice alone and with partners. Activity challenges can include:

1. In a space by yourself, practice tossing and catching by yourself. Choose a yarn ball or beanbag.
2. In your own space, practice throwing at the wall. Throw overhand as hard as you can.
3. Throw the ball to a high level, medium level, and low level.
4. Throw the ball to a partner. If you are successful, take a step back and throw again (Graham, Holt/Hale, & Parker, 1987; Nichols, 1990).

As children grow, these challenges can become more complex.

Activities which characterize symbolic or make-believe play can easily be incorporated into all types of play experiences in various settings. Imagery problems which include a variety of movement concepts are both fun and challenging. Specific examples include:

1. Picture yourself in a tropical jungle. You are suddenly stuck in quicksand and slowly start to sink. Try to pull yourself out. How many different ways can you try to pull yourself out?
2. Pretend you are a snowflake. How do snowflakes move? Be a big puffy one. Try being an icy one.

Imagery stories which allow children to enact visits to a zoo or farm are also very enticing. In addition, children enjoy being objects such as bubbles, snowmen, and clouds.

As children become older and pass through the latter stages of cognitive development (Bammel & Bammel, 1982), their abilities to handle more complex games increase. Chasing, fleeing, and dodging activities, previously done with partners or in small groups, can be expanded to include more participants. Games involving kicking or striking may more closely resemble "real games." As children pass through developmental levels at different stages, it is vital to present options within activities which allow children to participate and be successful at a variety of developmental levels. Kicking games (Jolly Ball, Sideline Soccer, and Mini-soccer) may need to be modified further with a smaller playing area, different size ball, or player rotation, in order to accommodate all players (Pangrazi & Dauer, 1992).

Participation for the joy of playing and skill mastery are two aspects of the arousal-seeking and competence-effectance theories. Activities presented to children must be challenging, but must also be ones at which children believe they can be successful. Experts in the movement field (Graham, et al., 1987; Nichols, 1990; Orlick, 1982; Pangrazi & Dauer, 1992) advocate providing activities incorporating challenges which may be adopted as children acquire and master specific skills. An example of these points can be demonstrated with basketball activities.

1. Throw and catch with a partner.
2. Throw and catch so that you have to move to catch the ball.
3. Throw and catch while you and your partner are traveling.

Children can then be challenged to play a modified form of half-court basketball. Specifics might include having three players to a side and having players shoot the ball to the basket or pass to a teammate upon possession, with no dribbling or steps allowed. Further advances can be made with games such as Basket Endball which adds shooting chances or Zone Basketball, which focuses on a wider inclusion of basketball skills (Graham et al., 1987; Pangrazi & Dauer, 1992).

Softball activities are another example. In regulation softball, action is often limited and many children often do not get an opportunity to gain a sense of skill mastery. Orlick (1982) provided the following options to increase player enjoyment and advancement.

1. All bases count. Each time a player progresses to a new base, she earns a point for the team.
2. All positions: Every player has an opportunity to play every position.
3. All fielders touch: All fielders must make contact with the ball after it is hit in order to stop the runner.

Making challenges appropriate for children is a key aspect in creating meaningful play experiences. Elements of novelty and uncertainty are exciting; yet, these must be done in a manner which allows children to succeed.

Creating meaningful and beneficial play experiences is an essential task for professionals committed to providing a positive environment for children. Knowledge of play can help parents, child care providers, educators, and recreation leaders plan the best and most appropriate games and activities for children at levels which allow for maximum enjoyment and success.

References

Bammel, G. & Bammel, L. (1982). *Leisure and human behavior.* Dubuque, Iowa: W. C. Brown Co.

Bergen, D. (Ed.). (1988). *Play as a medium for learning and development.* Portsmouth, N.H.: Heinemann Education Books, Inc.

Bruner, J. S., Jolly, A., & Sylva, B. (Eds.). (1976). *Play: Its role in development and evolution.* New York: Penguin.

Csikszentimaihalyi, M. (1975). *Beyond boredom and anxiety.* San Francisco: Jossey-Bass.

Ellis, M. (1973). *Why people play.* Englewood Cliffs, N.J.: Prentice-Hall.

Froebel, F. (1887). *The education of man.* (W. N. Hailmann, trans.) New York: D. Appleton.

Frost, J. L. (1988). Child development and playgrounds. In *Play spaces for children: A new beginning.* Reston, Va.: American Association for Health, Physical Education, Recreation and Dance, pp. 3-28.

Frost, J. L. & Klein, B. L. (1979). *Children's play and playgrounds.* Boston: Allyn-Bacon.

Garvey, C. (1977). *Play.* Cambridge, Mass.: Harvard University Press.

Graham, G. Holt/Hale, S. A. & Parker, M. (1987). *Children mainly.* Palo Alto, Calif.: Mayfield.

Gulick, L. H. (1920). *A philosophy of play.* Washington, D.C.: McGrath.

Kraus, R. (1984). *Recreation and leisure in modern society.* New York: Appleton-Century-Crofts.

Neumann, E. A. (1971). The elements of play. Unpublished doctoral dissertation, University of Illinois.

Nichols, B. (1990). *Moving and learning.* St. Louis: Times Mirror/Mosby College.

Orlick, T. (1982). *The second cooperative sports and games book.* New York: Pantheon Books.

Pangrazi, R. P. & Dauer, V. P. (1992). *Physical education for elementary school children.* New York: Macmillan.

Piaget, J. (1962). *Play, dreams and imitations in childhood.* New York: Norton.

Rubin, K. D., Fein, G. G., & Vandenberg, B. (1983). Play. In E. M. Hetherington and P. H. Munsen (Eds.), *Handbook of child psychology, socialization, personality, and social development,* pp. 698-774. New York: Wiley.

Schiller, F. (1875). *Essays, aesthetical and philosophical.* London: Bell & Sons.

Sessoms, H. D. (1986). *Leisure services.* (6th ed.). Englewood Cliffs, N.J.: Prentice-Hall.

Smith, P. K. & Vollstedt, R. (1985). On defining play: An empirical study of the relationship between play and various play criteria. *Child Development, 56,* 1042-1050.

Spencer, H. (1873). *Principles of psychology.* New York: D. Appleton.

Spodek, B., Soracho, O. N., & Davis, M. (1987). *Foundations of early childhood education: Teaching three-, four-, and five-year-olds.* Englewood Cliffs, N.J.: Prentice-Hall.

Sponseller, D. (1974). *Players as learning medium.* Washington, D.C.: National Association for the Education of Young Children.

Sutton-Smith, B. (1970). A psychologist looks at playgrounds. In *Playground Equipment,* pp. 13-15. Educational Products Information Institute.

Toffler, A. (1980). *The third wave.* New York: William Morrow.

Webster's New Collegiate Dictionary. (1980). Springfield, Mass.: G. & C. Merriam.

M. Jean Keller, Ed.D., is a professor of recreation and leisure studies at the University of North Texas. Her background is in therapeutic recreation. Karen H. Weiller, Ph.D., is an assistant professor of kinesiology at the University of North Texas. Her background is in elementary physical education and sport sociology.

Chapter 19
From Theory to Practice:
Observing and Thinking about Children's Play

STUART REIFEL

Piaget defined play as "primarily mere functional or reproductive assimilation" (1962, p. 87). His primary interest was the acquisiton and structuring of knowledge, the process of equilibration that involves assimilation and accommodation. As we (adults and children) experience the world, we create mental structures through assimilating experience; when we act on something physically or encounter anything (including words) that we can sense, we take it in. Every so often, we encounter something that does not make sense; that is, it does not fit into the mental structures that we have assimilated so far. When we are challenged by this encounter, we try to make sense of it. If it forces us to alter our thinking, we change or accommodate structures. This process of adjusting to new information is equilibrium. Learning occurs when we accommodate our mental structures to meet the demands of new information that did not make sense to us before. Play, on the other hand, is primarily mere assimilation. It is performed for pleasure, provides a feeling of power or virtuosity, and alters reality to suit the wishes of the child. It is not, from Piaget's point of view, learning, imitation, or objective thought.

Piaget used a stage theory of play to describe play's role in symbol formation. He defined several stages which matched his stages of cognitive development: practice or functional play, primary during the sensory-motor stage of development during the first year-and-a-half to two years of life; symbolic play, dramatic and possibly construction activities during the pre-operational stage of development, during the second through seventh years of life; and games with rules, beginning with concrete operations at about age six or seven. It is interesting that he made use of some, but not all, of Buhler's (1935) categories of play. In other words, he built on an earlier theoretical framework that addressed play, but he built on only part of that framework. He took the parts that related to his interest in cognition, especially the parts that dealt with symbols, while not addressing any number of other aspects of play (language play, rough and tumble play, humor) that most people would agree are legitimately part of play.

Piaget was concerned with the development of cognition. His argument was that play, as one way of assimilating our understanding of symbols, is one of the primary cognitive activities of the early childhood years. (Remember, children are not "learning" symbols during this stage; they are exploring the creation and manipulation of symbols.) Symbolic play is clearly a cognitive activity for children, but the symbols that they acquire through play are personal symbols that they manipulate to their own ends; they are not socialized, objective symbols. We, as adults, must learn to recognize and interpret them.

When Piaget (1945) wrote about symbolic play, he was referring to transformations that the child is making for her own pleasure. The child is either transforming objects into something that they are not (e.g. pretending that a wooden block is an ear of corn), transforming herself into something other than what she is (e.g., pretending to be mommy), or both. *Play, Dreams and Imitation in Childhood* presents a theoretical description of the development of these transformations, including observations of child's play that illustrate the description. By adding the facts discovered in research that has built on this theory, we can outline a number of steps that can guide our curriculum planning for young preschoolers.

A number of studies have built on Piaget's theory by investigating the manner in which children symbolically transform objects and themselves as they play. Fein (1975) looked at the way that degree of resemblance between a toy and what it is "supposed" to be will facilitate pretend play in the late toddler years. In a number of studies, Watson and Fischer (1977) and Watson and Jackowitz (1984) looked at the number of pretend transformations that a child can perform as she grows older and at the developing sense of social role that is reflected in her pretend. By putting together these studies, based on Piagetian theory, with Piaget's observations, we can see the developmental steps in pretend play, as follows:

1. Between 12 and 18 months, a typical child will be able to transform one toy that resembles a real object (e.g., she can pretend to eat a toy banana; she can pretend to drink from an empty toy cup.)
2. Soon thereafter, a typical child will be able to transform a toy human or toy animal so that it will "act" (e.g., a stuffed animal will "bark;" a doll will "walk.")
3. By 18 months, a typical child will be able to transform a toy that does not resemble anything (e.g., a wooden block can be used as a car; a cup of sand can be called "soup.")
4. By two years, a typical child may transform herself into someone else, if there are realistic toys to support the play (e.g., with a doll and cloth, a child will act as if she were the mother putting a baby to bed.)
5. By age two-and-a-half, a typical child may be able to transform multiple realistic toys at the same time (e.g., with a toy tea set and dolls, a child may create a tea pary.)
6. By three years, a typical child may be able to transform herself into someone else, using non-represetational toys as props for the play (e.g., a child may make cakes in the sand, pretending to be a baker.)
7. By four years, with representational toys children may be able to transform themselves into a number of interactive roles (e.g., with toy fireman hats and a card board box, several children could pretend to be firemen putting out a fire.)
8. By four and a half or five years, children may create their own pretend props as they take a

variety of roles (e.g., children may build a farm out of blocks, make animals out of clay, then pretend to be farmers.)

Parten, like Piaget, has become a standard citation for those interested in play, although she is used when our interests are the social aspects of play. As with Piaget, Parten's primary interest is not play; rather, she was concerned with social relationships and how they develop, or as she put it, social participation (Parten, 1932). She was not trying to understand play; she was trying to understand how social interactions develop. It just so happens that children in the classrooms where Parten made her observations were playing (as children tend to do), so it is easy for us to assoicate her stages with play. Her stages of social interaction (unoccupied, solitary, parallel, associative, co-operative) have become a standard framework for understanding the play of preschoolers. This suggests how we must be careful about using her work to understand play, knowing that play was not first and foremost on her mind as she was trying to make sense of children.

Piaget and Parten, like other researchers who have studied children, give us some useful ideas that help us to understand play and incorporate it in classroom activities. I hope that the preceding discussion has shown that each of the commonly cited theorists can tell us something important about play, but they do not tell us everything that we might need to know in order to understand play. Piaget tells us only about those aspects of play that help children explore objects, symbols, and rules; he does not tell us about language, humor, or any number of other playful activities, nor does he tell us about learning that occurs during play. Parten tells us about the kinds of social interactions that can take place among individuals who play and how those interactions are likely to develop over time; she does not tell us about styles of social interactions, social status, or language use during play. Each of these theorists looks at a piece of the picture, and he or she looks at that piece in great detail. Neither of them can be seen to look at play in its rich entirety in a manner that can be comprehensive for practice.

Applying Theory to Practice: An Example

It is important that we not stretch theories about early childhood beyond their ability to account for play as it occurs among young children. Yet it is possible to make good use of theories, like Piaget's, as we support and encourage children's play.

The development of pretend play, as understood by Piaget, Fein, Watson, Fischer, and Jackowitz, suggests the kinds of materials that should be available to children of different ages. The kinds of materials that children have to play with should match their cognitive level of play. (We know that any one classroom will have children with a range of abilities, so it is probably a good idea to have materials that reflect two or three steps, as listed above, in any classroom.) Toddlers should have more toys that resemble real-world objects and some nonrepresentational toys. As they grow older, they should be able to play with more nonrepresentational materials, such as blocks, clay, and drawing materials.

Second, developmental stages of play give us norms that we can look to as we observe children play. Toddlers will demonstrate brief transformations of self or of objects; as children grow older, they transform themselves by taking roles; kindergarteners will take and sustain interactive roles. Again, any classroom will have children operating at a number of steps; that is what developmentally appropriate practice is all about.

This leads us to a third point. These steps can guide us in planning the materials and the kinds of play that we might want in classrooms. And they give us guidance for documenting children's growth and progress. As you watch each child over the course of the year, can you see progress from one step to the next? Is the number of transformations that a child makes as she plays increasing? (Some children may skip a step; some may move back and forth from one step to another, then progress to the next. Developmental patterns vary among children.) These are all bridges between theory and practice.

We can build a clear bridge from theory to practice in this look at Piagetian theory and research as it relates to classroom play. The theory and research give us steps that we can use in a number of ways to help us implement and understand what we practice. Children's behavior in the classroom tells us whether the theory does indeed carry over into practice.

Additional Points of View

Having seen some of the limitations of Piagetian theory as well as how it can help us shape practice, it is worthwhile to see how we can broaden our view of play. Knowing that Piaget deals with one rather well-defined but narrow aspect of play (its relationship to how we develop symbols), and knowing that Parten is concerned only with certain well-defined aspects of social relationships (the types of associations that we develop), what else is there that we might want to think about as we watch and plan for children's play? What other theoretical princples may be important for how we think about what children are developing as they play? As mentioned above, language development is one concern, as Garvey (1977a, 1977b) has shown. Likewise, humor may be important (Opie & Opie, 1959). Literacy is another subject that is increasingly associated with play (Christie, 1991; Miller, Fernie & Kantor, 1992). Friendship and other aspects of social development also have been studied by Corsaro (1985).

Many of us are becoming increasingly interested in Vygotsky's (1974) theory of play as it relates to socialization and cognition. His observations of how children use toys as "pivots" to assist them in pretend transformations may provide us with a view of cognitive play that complements Piaget's. He may tie play more to a social context (as Piaget does not) and link pretend play to our shared base of symbols (Reifel & Yeatman, in press).

Another theorist who has become increasingly important to those who study children's play is Bateson (1972). He created a theory of play that applies to humans and to other animals. For Bateson, play is "as if" behavior, when one acts in a way other than what is appears to be. We see this when cats play at fighting. We also see it when children pretend to fight or when we dance as if we were floating. What is important about play is that it involves the establishment of a frame; participants who play together (or someone who plays alone) use signals to indicate that "this is play." These signals

nals to indicate that "this is play." These signals are markers that establish the frame and let others know that what is in the frame is play.

Signals and frames are potentially important for a number of reasons. First, they should promote effective verbal and nonverbal communication. Second, they should expand our abilities to think about things in multiple ways and to deal with paradox. Third, they may allow us to meet our psychological needs by altering our frames of mind. And fourth, they may allow us to learn to adapt to the many roles (father, teacher, boss, organizational secretary, etc.) that we must take as human beings. These are significant aspects of human development that are not addressed in other play theories. Bateson's theory of frames supports a connection between play interactions and a range of other frames in children's lives (Yeatman & Reifel, 1992). For example, children playing together may establish a play frame that draws on their knowledge of spelling. A play frame may allow children, through play, to explore the nature of their power over one another. They may use play to probe the limits of social rules, as when it is acceptable to be naked. They also may use a play frame to further family traditions, such as telling stories. The roles and signals that children use as they play give them an increasingly clearer picture of who they are in the world.

Conclusion

Theories of child development address play in different ways. As we learn more about play, we will be able to establish more principles that can serve as steps or guides for planning curricula and assessing children. At this point, theories can enhance the understanding we form based upon our own experiences. This might help us make better sense of the very complex thing that we call play, in our minds (theory) and in our classrooms (practice).

References

Bateson, G. (1972). *Steps to an ecology of mind*. New York: Ballantine Books.

Buhler, C. (1935). *From birth to maturity*. London: Kegan, Paul.

Christie, J. F. (Ed.) (1991). *Play and early literacy development*. Albany, N.Y.: State University of New York Press.

Corsaro, W. A. (1985). *Friendship and peer culture in the early years*. Norwood, N. J.: Ablex.

Fein, G.G. (1975). A transformational analysis of pretending. *Developmental Psychology, 11,* 291-296.

Garvey, C. (1977a). *Play*. Cambridge, MA: Harvard University Press.

Garvey, C. (1977b). Play with language and speech. In S. Ervin-Tripp & C. Mitchell-Kernan (Eds.), *Child discourse*, pp. 27-48. New York: Academic Press.

Giffin, H. (1984). The coordination of meaning in the creation of a shared, make-believe reality. In I.Bretherton (Ed.), *Symbolic Play* (pp. 73-100), Orlando, Fla.: Academic Press.

Miller, S. M., Fernie, D., & Kantor, R. (1992). Distinctive literacies in different preschool play contexts. *Play & Culture, 5,* 107-119.

Opie, I., & Opie, P. (1959). *The lore and language of school children*. London: Oxford University Press.

Parten, M. B. (1932). Social participation among preschool children. *Journal of Abnormal and Social Psychology, 27,* 243-262.

Piaget, J. (1962). *Play, dreams and imitation in childhood*. New York: Norton. (Original work published in 1945).

Reifel, S., & Yeatman, J. (In press). From category to context: Reconsidering classroom play. *Early Childhood Research Quarterly*.

Vygotsky, L. S. (1974). *Mind in Society*. Cambridge, MA: Harvary University Press.

Watson, M. W., & Fischer, K. W. (1977). A developmental sequence of agent use in late infancy. *Child Development, 48,* 828-836.

Watson, M. W., & Jackowitz, E. R. (1984). Agents and recipient objects in the development of early symbolic play. *Child Development, 55,* 1091-1097.

Yeatman, J., & Reifel, S. (1992). Sibling play and learning. *Play & Culture, 5,* 141-158.

STUART REIFEL, ED.D., is an associate professor of curriculum and instruction at the University of Texas at Austin, where he is affiliated with the early childhood education program. His interests are in relating classroom play to theories of development.

Chapter 20
Assessing Cognitive Development
by Observing Children's Outdoor Play

Jill Englebright Fox

Many early childhood teachers practice observational assessments of play for the purpose of discovering cognitive development only when they and the children are inside. While they may observe evidence of social and physical development when the children play outside, teachers often overlook the potential for assessing cognitive development in the outdoors.

To test my theory that children's outdoor play can reveal cognitive development, I systematically observed four- and five-year-olds at a play-based preschool. The preschool prides itself on having a non-academic program. Emphasis is placed on social skills and discovery learning. Letters and sounds are touched upon in the four-year-old class through literature-based and art activities, but phonics mastery is not emphasized or even encouraged. Five-year-olds spend a little more time on phonics, but again emphasis is on reading for enjoyment and language experiences. Math skills for both ages include a focus on cognitive counting, one-to-one correspondence, and shape identification. The children in this program are not assessed for their mastery of either academic or social skills, but through observation and interaction the teachers manage to keep a fairly good picture of each child's abilities. This information is used in informal conferences to keep parents apprised of their children's activities and to point out any potential trouble spots.

I generally began my observations of the children at this preschool by sitting in an out-of-the-way location with a good view of the entire playground. During each observation, I focused on one particular group of children involved in a play activity. This strategy necessitated frequent movement around the playground as the children's play took them from one location to another. After completing eight observations in this manner, I asked two of the center's teachers to become key informants in interviews about their classes' outdoor play.

The playground is approximately 200 feet by 100 feet. Three sides are surrounded by a high wooden fence; the fourth side is bounded by the building itself. Pea gravel over a layer of sand covers the surface of most of the play environment. The area between the basketball goal and the building is surfaced with flagstone tile. Loose parts, those items in the play environment which are portable and can be used by the children for play in various locations on the playground, are generally stored in a small hut.

During my observations I looked for specific behaviors or verbalizations from the children that would give evidence of mastery or understanding of concepts in math, science, social studies, and phonics and literacy. After completing each observation and interview, I typed my rough field notes into a more finished form, supplementing my scribblings with remembered details that I had not had time to include while in the field. I made three copies of each set of typed observations and used the copies for coding my data analysis. The very nature of my study made coding a simple matter. Since I was looking for specific evidence of skills or knowledge in math, science, social studies, and phonics and literacy, I used these subject areas as coding catergories. During data analysis several other codes emerged, such as knowledge of school rules and routines, social skills, and sports. Because the focus of this research is on cogitive development, these categories are not discussed in this paper. Assigning each code a separate color, I organized according to vignettes various areas of skills and knowledge. Some incidents related to two or more subject areas. Analysis of these categories revealed that even though these children had not been exposed to an academic learning environment, their play gave significant evidence of their understanding of many concepts.

Math skills were particularly in evidence in their play. Cognitive counting, in which the children clearly associate the number with the objects being counted, was seen many times as children counted loose parts or the number of participants in their play activities. Miranda, a five-year-old who has not yet attended kindergarten, counted cognitively for me one afternoon as she made a "birthday cake" while playing in the gravel:

Miranda: "I'm going to put in more candles." Me: "How many more?" Miranda breaks a long stick into pieces. Miranda: "Eighteen, because he's going to be 18 on his next birthday." She begins to count her stick parts. Miranda: "I only have nine. I need some more sticks." She looks around under a nearby tree and finds two more sticks. She breaks these into pieces and then counts all of her "candles". Miranda: "I have 19—that's too many. Well, maybe he'll just be 19 today."

Miranda not only demonstrated her ability to count cognitively to 19, she also showed that she understands that 19 is bigger than 18. Such comparisons were common in my observations. Children compared the numbers of loose parts each was working with, the sizes of their respective butter tubs, the height to which they could jump or climb, and the speed with which they could run. Most often these comparisons were accurate. The children were able to compare concrete objects in size and number. When the comparisons became more abstract, such as those based on their own running speed, their accuracy frequently gave way to egocentricity and each child's desire to out do his or her friends.

One-to-one correspondence was another skill that was easily observed in children's play activities I was able to see this skill as children distributed loose parts or as they went about their dramatic play activities.

Lauren, Miranda, and Shauna are in the toy *hut* playing house. Lauren: "We can't sit down yet. We have to get our house cleaned up. You all help me!" Miranda: "Well, don't throw all of the chairs out. We need these." Shauna: "We need these." Lauren: "I need one, too. We have to put three down there so that each of us has somewhere to sit. Put three down there."

The children's knowledge of shapes was also easy to observe as they built roads and structures with waffle blocks and giant interlocking plastic blocks. Most often the children identified these shapes in the course of their play activities and through conversations with each other.

Several children also gave evidence of the ability to make accurate estimates of heights and size as they discussed how to fit blocks together to make a desired structure or how to fit a toy truck into a recently-built garage or bridge. The more abstract estimations of time, however, are clearly beyond the reasoning of the two five-year-olds in the following vignette:

Lauren and Jamie are baking birthday cakes for their teacher. They have mixed the batter and placed the cakes in the pretend oven under the balance beam. Lauren: "Now we have to wait for four hours." Jamie: "It takes a long time." They stand for a moment. Lauren: "Let's check it now." She stoops down and pulls her butter tub out from under the balance beam. She pokes her finger in it. "Yep, it's done."

Surprisingly, given the ages of the children involved, several children were able to perform addition problems in their play activities. This skill was performed unselfconsciously by the children, and even the teachers didn't seem to notice that through their play activities the children were correctly using some relatively complex math operations.

Ross, Cody, Jeremy and Luke are playing basketball. Ross has just made a basket and he and Cody are cheering. Ross: "Yeah, it's three to zip. We're winning!" The teacher walks over. Teacher: "Did he make a basket?" Cody: "He made two and I made one. That's three!" Teacher: "Oh, great!" The teacher steps back to watch as the game continues.

Evidence of literacy development, though much more subtle, was still clearly present in many of the children's play activities. Color recognition was present when the children indicated toy selections or stated preferences by naming the colors of the desired objects. On one occasion Laura and Lauren shared their knowledge of the similarities and differences between two particular words with me.

Lauren: (to me) "This is my friend. She's Laura. My name is the same as hers only I have an 'EN' and she only as an 'A'. Me: "I see. There's a big difference." Both girls nod their heads and then go back to their play activities.

Knowledge and understanding of prepositions was also visible in the children's outdoor play. Children followed their own directions for putting the blocks on or beside each other, for driving their trucks under the bridge, and for climbing up the ladder. Frequently, discussion involving prepositional knowledge also required the use of some problem-solving skills.

Four children have built a hopscotch board with the waffle blocks. The board intersects with one of the balance beams. The four children begin to hop along the board in a line. When Luke, the leader, gets to the balance beam he stops. Luke: "We've got a problem here! What can we do? We can go over it." Kelsey: "I can't jump that high!" Lauren: "We have to go under it, then." Kelsey and Lauren go around Luke as he watches them. Lauren crawls under the balance beam and continues to hop the rest of the board. Kelsey climbs on top of the balance beam and jumps off onto the board.

The children's dramatic play provided several opportunities to observe sequencing skills. Much of the outdoor dramatic play at this preschool was based on themes that were familiar to the children. They were knowledgeable about the multi-step routines their play imitated and were able to point out when a friend deviated from standard form.

Lauren and Jamie are baking gravel birthday cakes. Lauren: "Okay, that's enough stirring. Now we have to bake it." Jamie: "I'm going to put on the icing." Jamie picks up two handfuls of rocks and gets ready to add them to the rocks already in her butter tub. Lauren: "No, first you have to stir it, then you have to bake it in the oven, and then you can put the frosting on. Come on!"

In the area of social studies, the children demonstrated knowledge of very concrete concepts, such as what a firefighter does at the fire station and at the scene of a fire, or how a farmer feeds the chickens. The birthday cake was a recurrent theme during sand and gravel play, indicating the importance of birthdays in the children's minds. The children also demonstrated their knowledge of several more abstract concepts such as giving in to a friend in order to keep the peace, and knowing the difference between winning and losing a game.

Science was perhaps the most difficult academic subject of which to find evidence in the children's play. In only one instance did I hear or see the children working with science concepts.

Curt and Courtney are playing in the gravel. Curt is building a large rounded pile. He uses his fist to pound an indentation in the top. Curt: "I'm making a volcano and it's getting ready to explode! The lava will run down the sides and it'll be very hot. It's gonna make some new rocks."

Although I was able to find considerable information on the skills and abilities of the children through observation of their outdoor play, interviews with two of the teachers revealed that they had different objectives for this outside time. Both teachers emphasized that outdoor play time should be unstructured time for the children. The first teacher listed two primary objectives for outside play, those of "blowing off steam" and physical exercise for the children. She believed that the unstructured nature of their outdoor play periods did not contribute to the children's development of academic skills. When questioned about this she responded, "Oh, I don't do lessons or anything like that outside. This is free time for the kids to do what they want to do. I don't want to force kids to learn to read."

The second teacher felt that physical exercise was the primary objective for outside play. She felt that outside play helped children to develop positive attitudes about school because it was fun, and that it helped children develop certain social skills like sharing and taking turns. This teacher also emphasized the use of the outdoor play period as a "break" for the children: "I don't teach while we are outside. The kids just play with each other. You can't make a kid sit and learn all the time. They have to have a break."

Both teachers emphasized their own roles as observers in the outdoor play environment, but with the goal of assuring safety for the children, rather than assessing skills. When asked if she felt she could learn anything about the children by watching them during outdoor play, the first teacher gave examples of personality characteristics and social skills that could be observed. In answer to the same question, the second teacher said: "Yeah, you can learn what the kids are really like. You can see how they act when you're not right there with 'em. And I get to talk with them a lot more than when we're inside. They tell me stuff about their families and stuff."

In conclusion, the interviews with these two teachers indicate that the outdoor play environment is an under-utilized part of this early childhood program. These teachers believe that outdoor play has a valid role in the program but use it only as a respite from indoor activities, rather than as an extension of the early chilhdood classroom.

Through my observations in this outdoor play environment, I was able to find several specific examples of the children's knowledge or mastery of academic skills. These examples were identified with minimal difficulty, even though I was operating under conditions that are slightly handicapped as compared to those of early childhood classroom teachers. First, I had only a rudimentary knowledge of the program's curriculum. A classroom teacher would have been aware of each math or science concept that the children had discussed and experimented with in the classroom. That teacher would have been able to hone in on actions by the children that gave evidence of their understanding that I completely missed. Second, a classroom teacher would have known the children. I knew most of their names, having seen them daily in the class and at birthday parties, but I did not know them as well as a teacher who has spent six hours a day for the past nine months would know them. I probably missed many actions that indicated small steps of accomplishment by an individual child, steps that a teacher would haved noted and applauded along the way. Third, the observations of a teacher would have been ongoing and much more purposeful. I only observed eight times; in establishing a routine for recording my observations I probably missed significant parts of the children's play activities. Also, my observations were only to validate a personal theory, not to have an impact on a child's life. I was probably not as careful and consistent as if I planned to use this information to plan curriculum, determine placement, etc.

During my observations of these children at play outside, I discovered some things: Cody can add. Lauren can sequence. Curt knows that rocks can be formed by volcanoes. Clearly, observation in the outdoor play environment is a valid method of assessing cognitive development in an early childhood program. These observations can be performed unobtrusively, without intruding upon the children's activities and without placing children in a stressful testing situation.

JILL ENGLEBRIGHT FOX is a doctoral candidate and teaching fellow in early childhood education at the University of North Texas at Denton, Texas. She taught kindergarten and first grade in the Texas schools for eight years. Her research interests include play, early childhood assessment, and young children's construction of physical knowledge in the outdoor play environment.

Chapter 20
Analysis of Play Behaviors of Third-grade Children on Contrasting Playgrounds

Joe L. Frost
Shu-Chu Sylvia Yang
John Horney
Jui-Chih Chin
Sheng-Hsi Lin

The National Survey of Elementary School Playground Equipment (Bruya and Langendorfer, 1988) investigated 206 public school playgrounds in 23 states, finding that few pieces of contemporary equipment were present and that playgrounds were extremely hazardous. Similar findings resulted from the National Survey of American Preschools (Wortham and Frost, 1990). Few American children have the opportunity to experience comprehensive types of creative play identified with interconnected play structures. The results also indicated that research and improved playground designs since 1950 have been generally ignored by the public elementary schools included in this survey (Wortham, 1988). Studies of toddlers, kindergarten, first-, and second-grade children (Frost and Campbell, 1985; Frost and Strickland, 1985; Keesee, 1990) found that playgrounds designed to provide for a wide range of play, using contemporary equipment, are superior to traditional playgrounds in soliciting a wide range of play activities and in meeting children's developmental play needs. The present study related to older children (third grade) and employed additional research techniques (i.e., anecdotal data and qualitative analysis) in determining similarities and differences in children's play behaviors and equipment choices in private school contexts.

The purpose of this study was to answer two research questions:

1. How do social play behaviors and cognitive play behaviors differ between contrastive outdoor environments?
2. What play equipment choices do third-grade children make and how do these choices vary across the two play environments?

In addition, qualitative data were derived from anecdotal notes. These data were organized into four categories — motor development, social development, cognitive development, and language development — and analyzed using grounded theory (Strauss and Corbin, 1990).

Methodology

Two third-grade groups (34 children at Site A and 51 children at Site B) were observed at play. Site A was equipped with new, attractive, interconnected "Big Toy" play structures manufactured by Northwest Design Products Corporation. The equipment and play areas included two extensive composite structures, two strap-swing structures, one tire-swing structure, obstacle-course (fitness) structures, and a basketball court. The two composite structures at Site A included a variety of apparatus connected by platforms, different types of slides, climbers, tunnels, and upper-body exercise equipment including a track-ride, a horizontal ladder, and a ring trek. The obstacle-course equipment, located in the peripheral area around the composite structures, consisted of balance beams, parallel bars, a climber, chinning bars, and a sit-up board. A retaining border kept protective sand surfacing in place.

The play environment at Site B was traditional, containing old equipment including a composite handbuilt structure, seesaws, swings, chinning bars, monkey bars, climbing dome, slides, an "S" climber and an open space for organized games.

Data were collected by observational ratings, time sampling, and anecdotal records.

The coding instruments used were an adaptation of Rubin's (1977) modification of Parten's (1932) social play categories and the cognitive classifications of Piaget (Rubin et al., 1983). Moore (1992) further refined this instrument to include the characterization of play behaviors in a nested, hierarchical fashion as done by Rubin and others. The coding took place after 80% inter-rater reliability was established.

Each child was observed 12 times. The order of observation was determined by random se-

---

Definition of Terms

The social play types used in this research are defined as:

Solitary play: The child plays alone and independently from other children in the same area with toys that are different from those that are used by the other children in the area.
Parallel play: The child plays independently from other children near him. He uses the same toys as another child near him.
Associative play: A type of group play in which all members engage in the same or similar activities; there is no division of labor and no organization of the activity of two or more individuals around any material goal or product.
Cooperative play: The child plays in a group that is organized for the purpose of the activity itself. The child is striving to attain some competitive or common goal.

The cognitive play types used in this research are defined as:

Functional: Simple repetitive muscular movements with or without objects.
Constructive: Manipulation of objects to construct or create something.
Dramatic of symbolic: The substitution of imaginary situations for objects in pretend play events.
Games with rules: The child accepts prearranged rules to govern play.
Chase: The child is planning to chase or is actually chasing another child or children.

---

lection. Each observation was one minute long (locating child, observing, recording). The recorded data included both a checklist of play types and equipment choices and a brief anecdotal record elaborating the play behavior, including information to give deeper insight into the observed play event. The checklists of play types and equipment choices yielded frequency and percentage data used to compare the two play environments.

The anecdotal records were used for qualitative analysis. The investigators combined all anecdotal notes and analyzed these data by open coding and axial coding. *Open coding* is the process of breaking down, examining, comparing, conceptualizing, and categorizing data. *Axial coding* is a set of procedures whereby data are put back together in new ways after open coding, by making connections between categories. This is done by utilizing a coding paradigm between categories which involves conditions, context, action/interactional strategies and consequences (Strauss & Cobin, 1990).

Results

In this section, two research questions will be answered. The first is: How do social play behaviors, cognitive play behaviors and non-

Social Play	Site A	Site B
Solitary	16%	4%
Parallel	4%	18%
Associative	74%	12%
Cooperative	6%	66%

Table 1.

Cognitive Play	Site A	Site B
Functional	63%	28%
Dramatic	9%	7%
Constructive	1%	0%
Games with Rules	11%	65%
Chase	16%	0%

Table 2.

play behaviors differ between contrasting out-door play environments?

At Site A (Table 1), the prevalent social play pattern was associative (74% of all play) followed by solitary (16%), cooperative (6%), and parallel (4%). Children at Site B spent most of their social play in cooperative play (66%), fol-

lowed by parallel (18%), associative (12%), and solitary (4%).

At Site A (Table 2), the order of cognitive play patterns was: functional (63%), chase (16%), games with rules (11%), dramatic (9%), and

Equipment Choice	Site A	Site B
Ring trek	10.6%	0.0%
Deck	8.4%	2.5%
Tunnels	6.7%	0.0%
Track ride	6.5%	0.0%
Basketball court	6.3%	0.0%
Horizontal ladder	5.6%	1.0%
Under deck	4.3%	1.5%
Spiral slide	4.0%	0.0%
Chinning bars	3.8%	0.0%
Chain ladder	3.4%	0.0%
Sit-up bars	3.4%	0.0%
Strap swing	3.1%	16.0%
Tube slide	3.1%	0.0%
Double slide	2.8%	0.0%
Chain net climber	2.7%	0.0%
Wheel chair deck	2.7%	0.0%
Cube climber	2.5%	0.0%
Chain walk	2.4%	0.0%
Roll bar	2.2%	0.0%
Incline bars	1.9%	0.0%
Bridge	1.8%	1.0%
Ramp	1.8%	0.0%
Firefighter's pole	1.6%	0.0%
Coil climber	1.3%	0.0%
Parallel bars	1.2%	0.0%
Sand play area	1.2%	10.0%
Steering wheel	1.2%	0.0%
Balance beam	0.9%	0.0%
Horizontal tires	0.9%	0.0%
Bubble panels	0.8%	0.0%
Tic-tac-toe	0.4%	0.0%
Tire swing	0.4%	0.0%
Moving balance beam	0.3%	0.0%
Dome climber	0.0%	1.0%
Open space	0.0%	65.0%
Seesaw	0.0%	1.0%
Slide	0.0%	1.0%

Table 3.

Categories	Frequency	
	Site A	Site B
Motor Development	458	314
Locomotor	231	0
Upper Body	122	0
Gross Motor	36	314
Exploration	35	0
Balance	27	0
Fine Motor	7	0
Social Development	146	17
Game-initiation	60	0
Leadership	30	0
Prosocial	22	14
Turn-taking	19	0
Modeling	10	0
Antisocial	0	1
Isolation	0	2
CognitiveDevelopment	100	45
Transformation	38	0
Challenge	33	1
Observation	29	10
Exploration	0	1
Imitative Role Play	0	15
Make-believe	0	15
Language Development	51	23
Information	35	0
Questioning	22	0
Listening	12	0
Claims	11	0
Language Play	1	3
Command	0	3
Description	0	5
Discussion	0	7
Language Confusion	0	1
Make-believe	0	2
Problem-solving	0	2

Table 4.

constructive (1%). at Site B the cognitive play patterns were: game with rules (65%), functional (28%), dramatic (7%), constructive (0%), and chase (0%).

The second question was: What play equipment choices do third-grade students make and how do these choices vary across the two play environments?

At Site A (Table 3) the children chose a variety of play equipment. The most popular was the Ring Trek (10.6% of all choices). This was followed by the decks (8.4%), tunnels (6.7%), track ride (6.5%), basketball court (6.3%), horizontal ladder, (5.6%), under decks (4.3%), and spiral slide (4.0%). Selection of the other equipment ranged between 0.3% and 3.4%. On Site B only 25% of the play choices were permanent fixed equipment. Sixty-five percent were open space (organized games) in the sand area.

From the anecdotal notes (Table 4), numerous categories were generated through axial coding procedures. The data were combined into like characteristics: motor development, cognitive development, social development, and language development.

Through open coding the following categories were developed from the data recorded on Site A: locomotor skills, balance skills, and gross motor movement skills, fine motor movement skills, upper body movement skills, and exploration of movement. The data from Site B were recorded in one category: gross motor skills. These categories were combined through axial coding procedure into the larger category of motor development.

At Site A, there were 231 (50%) incidences of locomotor skills and 122 (27%) incidents of upper body movement. There was one subcategory in motor development on Site B, 314 incidents of gross motor movement. Subcategories of cognitive development for Site A were: transformation (38), observations (29), and challenge (33). Subcategories of cognitive development for Site B were: imitative role play (15), make believe (15), challenge (1), and exploration (1).

Social development was divided into the following subcategories at Site A: modeling (10), turn-taking (19), prosocial (22), leadership (30), and game initiation (60). Social development was divided into the following subcategories on

Site B: isolation (2), prosocial (14), and antisocial (1).

Language development subcategories at Site A included: language play (1), information (35), listening (12), questioning (22), claims (11). Site B had the following subcategories: command (3), problem-solving (2), description (5), discussion (7), language confusion (1), make believe (2). Site A had 69% of information-giving, while Site B had 52% of discussion and description.

Discussion and Implications

At Site A, the prevalent form of social play was associative (74% of all social play), and at Site B the most prevalent form was cooperative (66%). Both types (associative and cooperative) included sharing ideas, competing, assisting one another, etc. The generation and use of rules (rules-governed play) was more prevalent at Site B with practically all of the cognitive play categorized as cooperative. Rubin (1977) and others have collapsed cooperative and associative play categories to form one category called group play.

The wide range of exercise equipment at Site A solicited a large variety of play with overhead apparatus. About one-third of all equipment choices were overhead apparatus (rings, track ride, exercise bars). This was used for practice (repetitious), chase, and "follow the leader" games and usually involved two or more children playing together (associative play). The absence of variety of challenging exercise equipment at Site B resulted in children (particularly the boys) playing soccer (cooperative play) extensively. Group play (associative and cooperative) frequency was virtually identical on the two playgrounds (80% at Site A; 78% at Site B). These third-grade children demonstrated high levels of group (associative/cooperative) activity but the equipment (or lack of equipment) tended to influence heavily the play activities chosen.

The solitary/parallel play frequency was also virtually equal at Site A and B (Site A 20%; Site B 22%). In sum, it appears that the type of play that third-grade children engage in is relatively consistent across contrasting play environments despite the content (equipment) or layout (structures, open areas, etc.). This pattern

Figure 1: Site A.

Figure 2: Site A.

Figure 3: Site B.

Figure 4: Site B.

is consistent with earlier research (Frost and Campbell, 1985; Frost and Strickland, 1985; Keesee, 1990; Winter, 1983; Moore, 1993) with toddlers through third-graders. Children across age groups play with whatever is available. The critical issue of *quality* of the play that does occur across contrasting ecological settings or play environments becomes a compelling issue.

One clue to quality of play is the type and range of cognitive play engaged in by children. At Site A, most of the play was coded "functional" because the dominant activity was using exercise-type equipment. Much of the play followed a chase game format in terms of children following or chasing one another around the linked equipment. Rules, though not evident in discussion and not coded as "games with rules," appeared to be inherent in the activity.

Another indicator of quality of play is the range of play and balance of play equipment used. At Site A, the children used 36 different equipment options, each providing a different challenge and collectively allowing an extensive range of motor development functions and play opportunities. At Site B, the children abandoned the relatively sterile, limited-play equipment to play in the open field and in the sand area under and around the equipment. Although not reported in this paper, gender data show that the dominant activity of boys at Site B was playing soccer while that of girls was sitting in the swings and role-playing in the sand area. At Site A, boys and girls engaged in equal amounts of functional and dramatic play while boys engaged in more games with rules (15% of all games with rules vs. 8%) and girls engaged in more chase games (19% vs. 12%). The quality of play was clearly superior and more equivalent for girls and boys at Site A.

Adults appear to select play equipment on the basis of tradition rather than play value. Examining the equipment play choices of children yields interesting results. For the third-grade children in this study, five of the 10 top choices were overhead exercise apparatus. The decks and tunnels were frequently used in chase and dramatic play. The basketball court was popular for organized games, and the very challenging spiral slide was among the top choices. Climbers dominated the next lower 10

choices — various types of equipment that provided access to and exit from decks and were linked for continuity of movement. Generally, the more challenging the equipment, the more it was used. The least-chosen equipment included bubble panels and tic-tac-toe. There is no challenge in a bubble panel (although supervision is enhanced by their use) and tic-tac-toe and other "academic-related" devices appear to capture little interest of children in outdoor play. Perhaps children wish to abandon the memory of classrooms during free play.

Anecdotal Notes

Qualitative data (anecdotal notes) and analysis offer even deeper insight into play quality than do quantitative data. Half of the larger category of motor development at Site A was locomotor skills. The challenges presented by the equipment encouraged rapid movement throughout the composite structure. The track ride, ring trek, exercise bars, and climbers encouraged upper body movements, which is the second most noted motor development category at Site A. The children at Site B, for the most part, ignored the equipment, choosing to engage in games with rules. Gross motor activity was the only type of motor development observed on this playground, evidenced primarily in soccer (boys) and swinging in the swings (girls). The key finding regarding motor development is that of *balance*. Site A children engaged in a range of motor activities, involving all parts of the body—locomotor, balance, gross motor, fine motor, upper body, and exploration (e.g., using exercise equipment in novel ways). The motor activities of Site B children were relatively stereotyped and limited.

Within the category of "cognitive development," Site A children engaged in more transformations, observations and challenges than were observed at Site B. The obvious reason for this was the wide range and complexity of equipment at Site A compared to Site B.

There was more role play and make believe play at Site B than at Site A. As children enter the concrete operations stage (Piaget, 1962) at about six or seven years, symbolic play decreases. However, when symbolic play materials are available to children they continue to engage in such play through the primary grades, although with less intensity over time. Neither Site A or Site B were designed to stimulate symbolic play and little was seen at Site A. Children were preoccupied with the wide range of motor challenges, consistent with the intent of the equipment designers and engaged in little symbolic play. At Site B, some children did not choose to play soccer or to use the equipment and retreated to the sand for symbolic play, using creative schemes and contrived or found materials. Earlier research in primary grades (Frost and Campbell, 1985; Frost and Strickland, 1985) shows that children continue to engage in symbolic play when symbolic play materials are available.

In social development, the Site A equipment lent itself to a wider range of social activities than did the Site B equipment. Activities at Site B were primarily prosocial but there was little opportunitiy for variety for soccer was the dominant activity. Since the Site A children were constantly varying their equipment choices and types of play, opportunities for socialization-modeling, turn-taking, leadership and game initiation were frequent.

Balance and variety of play were also evident in the children's discussion play. Site A children engaged in a wider range of language activities including seeking information, attentive listening, questioning, and making claims. Less language was coded for Site B children because it was difficult for the observers to get close enough to hear the language of children during soccer games and because some of the children were relatively silent during soccer games.

Conclusion

Social and cognitive play behaviors are heavily influenced by the type and variety of equipment and materials on playgrounds. While the cognitive play behaviors differ substantially across play environments, the overall social play behaviors are remarkably similar. However this similarity is seen for broad categories (e.g., solitary, parallel, group) only. There is considerable variations between playgrounds on specific activity within a category. Anecdotal notes indicate much greater variety and higher qual-

ity of play at Site A on both social and cognitive forms.

Obviously, children play with equipment and materials that are available. The wide range of equipment at Site A solicited much more balanced play (play across a range of equipment) and greater variety in play than was seen at Site B. Analysis of the anecdotal notes show that this translated into more indications of motor, social, cognitive, and language development for the children at site A than at Site B. Overall, the evidence favors the more comprehensive (Site A) playground over the traditional (Site B) playground for promoting broad forms of play and for enhancing child development.

References

Bruya, L. D. & Langendorfer, S. J. (1988). *Where our children play: Elementary school playground equipment*. Reston, Va.: American Alliance for Health, Physical Education, Recreation and Dance.

Chiang, L. (1985). Developmental differences in children's use of play materials. Unpublished doctoral dissertation. The University of Texas at Austin.

Frost, J. L. (1992). *Play and playscapes*. Albany, N.Y.: Delmar.

Frost, J. L. & Dempsey, J. D. (1991). Playgrounds for infants, toddlers, and preschoolers. In B. Brizzolara (Ed.), *Parenting education for school-age parents*. Lubbock, Tex.: Home Economics Center, Texas Tech University.

Frost, J. L. & Campbell, S. (1985). Equipment choices of primary-age children on conventional and creative playgrounds. In J. L. Frost and S. Sunderlin (Eds.), *When children play*. Wheaton, Md.: Association for Childhood Education International.

Frost, J. L. & Strickland, E. V. (1985). Equipment choices of young children during free play. In J. L. Frost and S. Sunderlin Eds.), *When children play*. Wheaton, Md.: Association for Childhood Education International.

Keesee, L. H. (1990). A comparison of outdoor play environments for toddlers. Unpublished doctoral dissertation, The University of Texas at Austin.

Moore, M. R. (1992). Analysis of outdoor play environments and play behaviors. Unpublished doctoral dissertation, The University of Texas at Austin.

Moore, N. V., Evertson, C. M., & Brophy, J. E. (1974). Solitary play: Some functional considerations. *Developmental Psychology, 10,* 830-834.

Parten, M. (1932). Social participation among preschool children. *Journal of Abnormal Psychology, 27,* 243-269.

Piaget, J. (1962). *Play, dreams and imitation in childhood.* New York: W. W. Norton.

Rubin, K. H. (1977). The social and cognitive value of preschool toys and activities. *Canadian Journal of Behavioural Science, 9,* 382-385.

Rubin, K. H., Fein, G., & Vanderberg, B. (1983). Play. In P. H. Mussen & E. Hetherington (Eds.), Handbook *of child psychology* (4th ed.), pp. 694-774.

Strauss, A. & Corbin, J. (1990). *Basic qualitative research: Grounded theory procedures and techniques.* London: Sage Publications.

Winter, S. M. (1983.) Toddler play behaviors and equipment choices in an outdoor playground. Unpublished doctoral dissertation. The University of Texas at Austin.

Wortham, S. C. & Frost, J. L. (1990). *Playgrounds for young children: National survey and perspectives.* Reston, Va.: American Alliance for Health, Physical Education, Recreation and Dance.

Wortham, S. C. (1988). Location, accessibility, and equipment on playgrounds. In L. D. Bruya & S. J. Langendorfer (Eds.), *Where children play: Elementary school playground equipment.* Reston, Va.: American Alliance for Health, Physical Education, Recreation and Dance.

Joe L. Frost, Ed.D., is Parker Centennial Professor of early childhood education at The University of Texas at Austin. He is the author of Play and Playscapes (Delmar, 1991) and also the author, co-author, editor, or co-editor of more than 100 books, reports, monographs, and articles in early childhood education. SHU CHU SYLVIA YANG, JUI-CHIH CHIN, and SHENG-HSI LIN are doctoral students in early childhood education at the University of Texas at Austin. JOHN HORNEY is a doctoral student in foreign language education at the University of Texas at Austin.